A Perfectly Logical Explanation

By Michael Chevy
Castranova

Library of Congress Control Number: 2002115177

Cover design by Dave Lambrix

Cover photograph by Lisa Williams

Preface

A Perfectly Logical Explanation for What You Are About to Read

When I was in the eighth grade, I fell from the second floor of a house. It wasn't an especially tall house. But the fall was far enough.

As I was about to start on the final chapter of this collection, I remembered that falling sensation — just all of a sudden, as an unexpected current of air.

Maybe it's because writing and falling off a house are very similar endeavors. You're fairly certain where you're going, but you don't know for sure how you'll feel when you get there.

I have to say, though, I feel pretty good about the stories here. Yes, I have changed the names of some of the people involved. That wasn't to make fun of them so much as to allow them plausible deniability.

But the adventures related here are all true. Or, as David Sedaris, the darling of National Public Radio, once replied when asked if everything in his essays were really true, it's all true enough ….

Most of the action in these essays — for that is what they're intended to be, even if obliquely — takes place in and around one of three metropolitan areas: Youngstown and Columbus, Ohio, and Kalamazoo, Michigan. The first city is where I was born, the second is probably where I grew up and the last is where I live now.

Chapters in the "Tales From the Home Front" series are set in Kalamazoo. Something very much like them (*these* have been augmented) — as well as "Cotton Club," under a different title — first appeared in *Business Direct Weekly*, the business-to-business newspaper I edit. (See, when you're the editor, you can run your own stuff.) "Safety First," with some alterations and with a different title, was first printed in *Columbus Monthly* in February 1995 and appears here with permission.

As for the book's title, it's the catch phrase they always seem to recite in sitcoms on television, when one character tries to explain some inexplicable situation another character has happened upon: "There's a perfectly logical explanation for all this …."

As in many of the occasions described in this collection, that was just the phrase I was looking for.

— *Michael Chevy Castranova*
November 2002

To Lisa, my primary and first reader

Contents

Chapter One
Judgment Day

When I was growing up, my father managed a shoe store in downtown Youngstown called Wilson's. Wilson's therefore always was referred to in our family as my father's store.

So until I got to the first grade, I thought my name was Mickey Wilson. On that first day of school, our teacher went around the room calling out our names. Imagine my surprise when she insisted my name in fact was not Wilson. Instead, she said, it was this name that was incredibly … well, long.

And I had already learned how to spell Wilson.

That, as it turned out, was only the first of many traumatic experiences during my eight-year prison sentence at the school we affectionately called St. Torquemada of the Bleeding Knuckles.

I'd once thought about making a movie about our school and my confinement there. But then I realized it already had been made. It was called *Stalag 17*.

It's little exaggeration to compare those eight dismal years at St. Torquemada in the early 1960s to being in a World War Two prison camp. We had uniforms, were kept to a strict schedule and were served rations only sparingly. Corporal punishment was meted out liberally, and we had little contact with the outside world. And we had warders — the nuns of St. Torquemada.

Even as a young child, I figured our teachers' heavy, cumbersome black garments — worn all year round, no matter what the weather — and the stiff, starchy wimples — those broad collars and pinching headbands — surely had a lot to do with their demeanor.

Our teachers were, for the most part when I attended St. Torquemada, in a word, old. As in ancient. And they didn't seem very happy in their chosen professions.

Why else would they insist we write with cartridge pens (yes, ball-point pens had been invented by this time), then penalize seven-year-olds for getting ink blotches on our homework? (Not to mention on our desks, on our clothing, on our fingers and in our hair.)

And surely they were frustrated. They must have been. After all, we had large classes — 150 some students in my first grade alone, divided into three groups. Moreover, the building in which we all daily labored was two solid-looking stories of tannish, flat masonry, the first floor actually with its windows at sidewalk level, to give us a clear view of the front tires of parked automobiles.

And, as St. Torquemada wasn't exactly an affluent school, our textbooks were so out of date as to be nearly useless — our geography books were copyrighted in 1938. There was little point in reading about Europe, say, or Africa … or much of the rest of the world, including even most of this country. The main industry in the South, according to our texts, was picking cotton. Germany was a wonderful country to visit as everything there was so orderly … and clean. And there was that nice man, Mr. Hitler ….

The nuns, it must be noted, preferred to be called sisters, as in Sister Mary Gertrude, Sister Mary Philodendron, Sister Mary Titus Andronicus …. The main weapon of choice of every sister at St. Torquemada was the yard stick. (I don't mean a measly old twelve-inch ruler, mind you — I'm talking about your good-sized, three-foot-long sturdy wooden stick that easily could be used in either a downward chopping motion — WHACK — or backhanded to the base of an offending grade-schooler's skull — WHACK.) On occasion, foot-long coils of chain-mail rosary beads worn about the waist also could be employed to deliver that spontaneous but meaningful smack across the hands — WHACK.

(You also probably can see why when, during a brief flirtation with fund-raising by charging us pupils for attending a command showing of the 1945 Bing Crosby wheezer *The Bells of St. Mary's*, and Sister Mary Pachyderm, the principal, touted the movie over the intercom as featuring "lots of nuns, lots of priests and lots of laughs," my friend Barty and I looked at each other in complete bafflement. “Lots of nuns” + “lots of priests” = “laughs”? Say what? Surely this movie took place in a reality different than ours ....)

The sisters were not alone in running St. Torquemada with a tight hand. They in turn answered to the sole male authority figure at St. Torquemada, the Monsignor.

The Monsignor was supreme ruler, and the nuns were just as afraid of him as we were. He was even older than our teachers, rotund — picture Alfred Hitchcock, except without the droll humor — and loud. He had a voice you could hear for miles. He didn’t speak — he boomed.

On Saturdays, when he would hear confession, parishioners would stand in line for any other priest on duty rather than go to the Monsignor. One reason was because the old man was famous for handing out extraordinarily severe penances — 400 Our Fathers, 6,000 Hail Marys and loss of your index finger. But the other was his thundering voice carried out of the confessional and within easy earshot of anyone within the confines of the county lines: “You had impure thoughts about *who*? You’ll burn in *hell*, young man ....”

The Monsignor also held our individual fates captive as he insisted on personally handing out reports cards — slowly and painfully — to each child, vigorously chastising anyone who dared get a low grade in the important subjects (that is, religion. We surely couldn’t be blamed for not knowing where the heck Brazil might be).

So four times a year, when we knew the cards were marked and ready, we waited in our classrooms, sometimes for days, heads bowed and hardly daring to breath, waiting for the Monsignor to arrive. We were petrified.

Then we’d hear him. Down the hall. Shhh. Is he coming here? Our teacher would hesitantly open the classroom door and brave a glimpse out in the hall. No, he’s gone in the other direction. Maybe he’ll come to our room tomorrow.

Then, without warning and with a boom like cannon fire, he’d storm into our classroom, kicking the door open with a crash, bellowing, “It’s Judgment Day.”

It is amazing any of us lived through the experience.

Our teachers and the Monsignor were united in their apparent narrow view of their charges. Most of us in the student body were about less than half their size. But they considered us constant schemers, tricksters who thought of nothing else during those long hours of confinement in St. Torquemada but of escape.

Which, of course, was true.

Most of the trouble occurred where we were most likely to flee — the playground.

Now, don't be misled: It was a playground only in the minds of our keepers. This "playground" was blacktopped, with regularly demarcated yellow rectangles painted on it. Cars rested on it for most of the day. No jungle gyms, no slides, no swings were in evidence. To all outward appearances, it would more likely be seen as … a parking lot.

It was to this playground/parking lot, which was built on a slight but noticeable incline, we students were marched out each midday, right after we had quickly devoured our cold bag lunches brought from home, for forty-five minutes of fun and frolic.

The sisters kept watch from the second floor, maintaining vigilance for fights that frequently broke out, and for the overactive children who couldn't help but run — and fall, invariably flailing several inches of skin off their arms, knees and faces as they skidded some distance down along the blacktop, their bodies coming to rest under one of the parked cars.

The teachers on guard also acted as spotters for the runners — the eight- , nine- and ten-year-olds who could stand it no more and had to make a break for it, hoping to dash across the roadway and find safety at the nearby shopping plaza.

When a youngster would make a break for freedom — and we'd all see him, like a desperate squirrel bolting across a busy highway — the alarm would sound, and a pair of nuns would be dispatched to give chase, their black capes billowing behind them as they bore down on their prey.

The rest of us would shout encouragement to our fleeing comrade … only to see him dragged back, sooner or later, sobbing, between the two retrieval-nuns who'd caught him.

In the first grade, I actually made it as far as Glenwood Avenue, well beyond the plaza, before being captured. It was winter, I recall, and as we were being marched out from morning church service — oh, yes, church was just about every day, as it was adjacent to the school building itself — I slipped out of line and ducked behind some bushes. As the column of children trooped past, I waited my chance, teeth chattering, the straps of my cap snapped securely under my chin. Then, once they'd disappeared around the corner, I made my escape.

But the problem with my plan was that, well, it wasn't planned much beyond that initial leap to freedom. I couldn't go home, could I? My mother would wonder why I was watching television at 9:15 a.m. on a Monday. And there were rumors that the merchants at the shopping plaza kept an eye out for escapees and would telephone the school.

So, as it turned out, as I wandered aimlessly about a quarter mile from my house, dithering over what to do next, one of our neighbors called the school and I was picked up shortly thereafter. And soon after that — WHACK.

Those students who didn't try to escape or get into fights or fall down mostly just stood around. In winter we huddled in groups, often up to our little hips in snow, as St. Torquemada didn't waste money on having the playground plowed. In summer, on the hottest days, we melted.

And for whatever reason, on the coldest of winter days and on the scorchingest of summer afternoons, Sister Mary Pachyderm — for whatever loopy reasons — would announce over the outside speaker to our uncomprehending ears that, as it was such a glorious day, recess today would be extended.

Once, when the temperatures were nearing 100 and our principal again had announced an incomprehensible extension of recess, a large block of students unstuck their feet from the sticky blacktop and, in a phalanx, rushed the main doors. Eighth graders, the school's official monitors, tried to barricade the entrance from the inside, holding on to the doors' handles for dear life. But we were too many for them and we would not be denied.

With only minimal casualties, we wrenched open the doors — a couple eighth-grade girls who hadn't let go of the handles soon enough were inadvertently chucked out onto the parking lot in the process — and we swarmed the water fountains.

We were punished within an inch of our young lives. But it was worth it.

Chapter Two
Going in Circles

Somewhere around our freshman or sophomore year in high school, I think, my friend Barty got his hands on one of those books intended to help increase your word power. He bought the book, I'm certain, not so much to improve his vocabulary as to impress girls. I can conceive of no *other* reason why he'd do such a thing.

Every day Barty would add two words from the book to his general conversation. Words such as obsequious and pandurate. He didn't actually bother to learn the *meanings* of these words. He'd just use them, dropping them into his sentences however and wherever the notion struck him.

"This sandwich tastes very obsequious," he would say. Or, in combination, "Let's obsequiate the pandurate."

After a very short while — maybe less than a week — Barty no longer bothered to add any *new* words. He just kept using the same half-dozen multi-syllabic bon mots over and over — and never with much precision.

And it was at the Rollercade where Barty found the best use for his new-found word power. Because it was to the Rollercade we went every Friday evening, in the late 1960s, for the absolute sole purpose of meeting girls.

The Rollercade was the ideal location for running into — yes, sometimes literally, and at high speed — a cross-section of young womanhood. A big old red barn-like structure, it was (and may still be) situated on Youngstown's far southeast corner, almost on the Pennsylvania border, and so attracted high-schoolers from a variety of neighborhoods.

So every Friday, as soon after supper as we could manage, we'd peel on our bathtub-shrunk-while-wearing-them-so-as-to-be-skin-tight faded blue jeans (everything back then was about hormones, surely) and made our way to the Rollercade. Neither

Barty or I were old enough to drive, and we preferred to have Barty's father take us — even in his rattling old gray Ford Falcon — rather than my parents, as we knew he'd be late picking us up.

Of course, one of our first challenges at the Rollercade was that neither of us had ever been on roller skates in our lives — and wearing skates was the primary rule there. No skates, no loitering. Our very first visit to the Rollercade, in fact, ended a matter of 10 minutes or so later when we were abruptly cast out, after we'd refused to put on skates.

We had a very long wait that first night, sitting outside in the parking lot, until Barty's dad came trundling back some four hours later. (We hardly could have telephoned him at home — likely catching him just as he walked in the door — to plead for him to turn around and pick us up as we'd just been physically ejected.)

So we learned to skate.

As the weeks went by, we could see right off there were two classes of skaters at the Rollercade — those who owned and those who rented. Barty and I were definitely renters.

The two owner-managers of this establishment had their own clear division of labor. One of them sat high up above the skating rink, along the north wall, where he played the organ with elaborate relish, elbows flailing giddily. Not that any of his tunes were in the least bit recognizable, but he did seem to enjoy himself.

The other owner — clad year-round in a heavy bright red sweater with silhouettes of deer on it — spent the evening skating around the rink, round and around, his head down, endlessly searching for loose change and gum wrappers on the floor, and muttering to himself about the complete worthlessness of teenagers the world over.

Alternating with the organ music was, well, real music. The Sixties, you recall, was known for two big things: the Vietnam war and the music … and all that they brought with them. And the music played out of the speakers at that Rollercade was perfect for that time and — we believed — for romance.

I'll bet I remember a good portion of the lyrics to just about every one of those songs: *I Think We're Alone Now*, sung by Tommy James and the Shondells, *Hey Baby They're Playing Our Song*, by the Delfonics, the Four Tops's *Bernadette*, *I Wonder What She's Doing Tonight*, by Tommy Boyce and Bobby Hart, *How Can I Be Sure*, from the Young Rascals (they didn't become the Rascals — without the Young part — for a couple more years), Otis Redding's mournful *Sittin' on the Dock of the Bay* and Mel Carter's tender *Hold Me, Thrill Me, Kiss Me*, anything by the Turtles (whose demise in the rock-and-roll world, I've always been convinced, could be dated from their acceptance to perform at Tricia Nixon's wedding), from *Happy Together* and *She's My Girl* to *Elenore* and *You Showed Me* — their music simultaneously up-tempo and distinctly melancholy. And possibly the most sublime of all, Johnny Nash leisurely but assuredly making his way through Sam Cooke's *Cupid*.

Yes, I know, the titles of these songs sound a little sappy now. OK, very sappy. But then, right then, at that Rollercade, those lyrics said exactly what we believed we wanted to say, and the arrangement of the tones made us feel precisely how we thought we should feel.

Many of the young people at the Rollercade those nights amazingly soon would get married, go off to university or to work in the steel mills — as their fathers, grandfathers and great-grandfathers had done — or be shipped off to Southeast Asia. But on those evenings, we thought about none of those things.

And, as the lights would dim and Frankie Valli would croon the opening bars of *Can't Take My Eyes Off of You* — or Peter Noone of Herman's Hermits would gently begin *There's a Kind of Hush* — we'd run our long-handled combs through our hair one last time, check our eager reflections in one of the floor-length mirrors, then softly sidle up to the fresh-faced girls we'd had our eyes on all evening. … And then Barty would say something like, "Shall we accentuate your verisimilitude …?"

Now, you might be surprised how frequently his bizarre verbal rapprochement actually worked. He'd keep chatting and, sometimes yes and sometimes no, manage to convince the girl to glide off to one of the benches, back in the darker corners of the building. (I usually did all right, too, though unlike my pal I generally contained my remarks to recognizable English.)

So there we'd be — boy and girl — sitting on one of the wooden benches and just working our way around to some serious making out when, inevitably and unalterably, the man in charge of keeping order at the Rollercade would appear, as if out of the shadows. His name was Officer Friday and he meant business. And that meant no smooching.

By way of enticement to see things his way, Officer Friday would crack his multi-purpose cubit-long flashlight against our exposed kneecaps. WHACK.

The girls would get off scott free, rolling away out of sight and out onto the rink. But as for the boys, as we sat there rubbing our aching patellas, Officer Friday standing over us, clenched fists on his hips, and bellowing, "Get skating or get out."

So we'd skate. To the Lemon Pipers, the Union Gap and the Buckinghams, to Spanky and Our Gang and to Billy Joe Royal's *Cherry Hill Park*, to the Box Tops singing *Cry Like a Baby*. To that incredibly awful organ music. Until we saw our next opportunity, maybe with the same girl or perhaps with someone else we'd seen before or who had just come in. We were, after all, on a mission. It was for *l'amour* we had come.

Not that all our outings at the Rollercade were always so clear cut. Once I'd foolishly made a date to meet two different women there on the same night. And they both showed up. Things got complicated for me.

Fortunately it was a very large place, and I managed to keep both dates — as long as I kept them at two different ends of the moving flow of skaters — me zooming from one to the other, back and forth, until quite a ways into the evening. Things did not end well, as I probably could have predicted myself had I not been so taken with the notion of two dates at once. And, boy, was I tired the next day from all that shuttling back and forth.

But the worst night was undoubtedly the last date Barty had with Darla. The pair had been meeting for several Fridays in a row and, even though she indeed had mentioned early on that she possessed a boyfriend, neither Darla or Barty were particularly worried. After all, Angel hated roller skating. He'd never show up at a place like this.

Events had been proceeding nicely. Barty and Darla had spent much of the night trying to avoid Officer Friday's vengeance and get in some pleasurable kissing, and I had been chatting up a girl named Geri. She went to the Catholic high school on the north side and wore a very short skirt, even for those days.

One of Darla's friends rolled over to tell her she'd heard through the grapevine that Angel had found out about her and Barty and was, to put it mildly, homicidally, insanely angry. That is to say, he was pretty darned upset.

Barty told me about the warning and, foolish boys that we were, we laughed. Angel? How could anyone be seriously afraid of any guy called Angel?

It was about an hour or so later when — as if in some community theater rehearsal for *Oklahoma* — whispers started to make their way across the Rollercade, building louder and more audible as the sounds got closer to us. "… Angel's here." "Angel's here." "*Angel's here.*"

And there, suddenly and for all the world to view, was Angel: Standing at the front entrance, his dark eyes scouring the rink no doubt seeking out his Darla. Flanked by two exceptionally large friends each about the size of a Volkswagen. His black leather jacket draped over his broad shoulders. Unshaven and decidedly unhappy.

And Barty and I could see —even from across the building — just catching the glint from the entranceway light was the butt of a handgun sticking out from the waistband of Angel's pants.

It was at that moment we decided roller skating maybe wasn't for us after all.

As Angel and his bodyguards were between us and the main door, we rocketed for the far wall, then caromed off toward the shoe exchange. We flung off our skates and grabbed for our shoes.

By this time we'd been spotted and, as Angel and his buddies made their way toward us, Barty and I dashed back out onto the skating rink in our bare feet.

Officer Friday, immediately noticing a violation of the prime directive, came charging out after us, yelling, "Hey, get skates on or get out." The trio of thugs were right behind him.

We were *trying* to get out.

Somehow I lost Barty in the melee out on the rink, as in our mad haste we bumped into baffled skaters, in couples and in linked-arm groups, and unintentionally knocked people over and set off chain reactions of collisions and flying bodies.

In the bedlam, I fled back over toward the exit, only to halt in my tracks when I saw one of Angel's henchmen trotting over to the same destination to cut me off.

"*Bend me, shape me, an-nee way you wan-ant me*," the American Breed was singing.

I veered off to the right and headed straight for the coat check room. Not slowing down a jot, I vaulted over the counter and crashed at top speed into coats, coat racks and the coat check girl.

When I finally managed to separate myself from all the clothing, racks and coat hangers — and the coat check girl — I got to my feet and zoomed out the heaven-provided fire exit door at the back of the coat check room.

Barty and I met up about 10 minutes later at the nearby McDonald's and, as we caught our breath, contemplated some new activities for our future Friday evenings.

As I said, that was our last trip to the Rollercade. We found other, somewhat safer, pursuits. That is to say, other places to seek out girls.

So instead we went to more dances and football games. But the music wasn't the same. And it was never again quite as much … fun.

As Barty would have said, "May I fibrillate your macadamizer …?"

Chapter Three

Tales From the Home Front: Winter
I'm Thinking Condo

I am no longer enamored, I suspect, with this concept of home ownership.

This occurs to me as I stand on my recently purchased 20-foot aluminum extension ladder, in the dark, in the cold, in the four-feet-deep snow, trying to break off some of this formidable four- to five-inch-thick ice that cobra-like hugs the gutters of my house.

My tool of choice for this project is your average-sized household hammer. (A flame-thrower was my first choice, but I don't own such a thing and, deep down, I worry there might be a problem with that notion that I'm overlooking at the moment.)

My arms, not surprisingly, are tired by now as I've been at this for about an hour or so. My toes are wet and very cold. And I keep getting tiny bits of ice piercing into my face.

Once, the hammer actually leaps out of my hand — an obvious and desperate attempt to escape — and caroms off the dining room window. To my amazed relief, the glass does not break. ("Oh, look what we're serving for supper tonight, dear — chilled hammer.")

I don't think I'm enjoying this experience.

My wife and I bought and moved into this house in the autumn of 1998. It is our first. We called our broker and cashed in our life savings. We altered our vacation plans to now encompass a drive to a shopping mall in Battle Creek.

It is not the largest house I've ever seen, but it's big enough. And at the time of our purchase, it was about 76 years old. Considering I've no idea how to fix anything, I'll grant you the logic of our buying a three-quarters-of-a-century-old house might have been a little ill-conceived.

Yes, I have been told — more than once — owning one's

own home is the American dream. We want to support the local economy. And we no longer desire to suffer those annoyances of apartment dwelling.

Such as the downstairs neighbor's daughter's boyfriend abandoning his car in the driveway, thereby effectively blocking the only entrance to or exit from our parking lot. The noise — quite possibly identified by some with more diverse experience in such things as music — barging up from elsewhere in the building at a window-rattling volume and inevitably after 11 p.m. The greasy cooking odors and cigarette smoke wafting through the cold-air returns, permanently permeating our furniture and clothing. The neighbor's actively adolescent rottweiler that spent its off hours doing who knows what in our shared basement. The debate over precisely how much common sense really is required to remember to lock the communal outside door.

And then there was the next-door property owner's dead oak tree that fell on our cars during the previous October's ice storm, flattening my wife's long-loved Toyota beyond driveability. (You still could wedge yourself behind the steering wheel, with some concerted effort, but not without your head scraping the car's roof. Unless you were the height of your average second-grader.)

Yes, owning your own home is a charmed life.

You think I'm being unappreciative? Well, OK, we've been pretty lucky with this house … so far. The furnace was making very odd noises a couple weeks ago, but then just as mysteriously stopped. The garage door declined to unlock late one recent Saturday night, forcing me to gain access to my own home by way of a previously latched upper window (and proving to my wife the Sixties really weren't a figment of my imagination). The shower assembly sort of collapsed one evening while I was standing under it, hitting me on the head ….

I'd spent more time in hardware stores over the past three months than I had in my entire lifetime before. (Did you know they actually sell something called rags in a box? Couldn't you scrounge around in your house for rags you've already paid for?)

And there's this ice and snow experience. The melting water has found its way along the side of the chimney, through the attic and an upstairs closet and, finally, oh so aesthetically down through our living room ceiling.

My first thought was to call the landlord.

I see a new roof in our future. Maybe a new furnace, too. (They'll make for a cozy place to come home to, after that trip to the hardware store or the mall.)

About a week later I had to call in a SWAT team of snow removal professionals. I got their telephone number out of the classifieds listing in the daily newspaper, and they showed up — about four or five of them, each with a lit cigarette dangling from his lips — the next snowy afternoon.

They slammed their ladders along the side of our house, then up they charged, as if to take the place by siege. Once on the roof, with pick-axes and small hatchets, they attacked the ice, pounding at it in wild abandon.

They clearly enjoyed their work.

On the ground, another of their troupe used a long roof rake — a device I'd never seen before but immediately knew I'd have to have — to lug down huge mounds of snow at a time, each pile crashing to earth with a deep THUMP.

I could catch glimpses of the guys on the roof through the falling, swirling snow as they hacked away, moving ever upward, sure-footed as monkeys.

~

Come spring, it seems we experience almost continual rain. This is probably due to our being some thirty-five minutes from Lake Michigan. Instead of lake-effect snow, it's lake-effect rain, I guess. The state should change the motto on its license plates — Michigan: Land of Moisture.

A good deal of this rain finds its way through our living room ceiling. It is time, we realize, to deal with the roof.

I obtain three bids, each approximating what I paid for my last automobile. Trying not to faint, I ask one of the roofers who's shown up to see the problem of the leaking roof first-hand if he has any *other* suggestions. (I believe I have to trust his judgment, as he's a roofing professional and all, even though he has confessed to a fear of heights … an odd quirk, I figure, given his line of work.)

He offers a stop-gap measure: Maybe, he says, maybe the water is coming in around that old chimney. He'll send over one of his guys to go up on the roof and slather some tar-like stuff around the chimney's base. Maybe, he says, maybe that'll work.

A couple days later I telephone the roofer to ask when he's sending his guy over. He was there yesterday, the roofer replies. I assure him that's not the case. OK, the roofer says, I'll make sure he shows up if not this afternoon, certainly tomorrow.

Two days later I call the roofer again to ask when he's sending his guy over. But he was there yesterday, the roofer swears.

As I'm talking to the roofer on the telephone, I see out the window a pickup truck pulling up outside and someone getting out.

I tell the roofer his guy is here now and I'll call him back later.

When I get outside, I notice the fellow is drunk. Or he's fallen and hit his head recently. Either way, he is very red in the face and weaving. Plus the fly of his pants is down.

He confesses that indeed he is the roofer's guy and he's here to set things right with the chimney. He lines up his ladder and, with cigarette firmly affixed between his lips, he wobbles his way up onto the roof.

About a moment later a woman appears. She also is smoking a cigarette. She is wearing very short shorts and carries a bucket of tar in her hands. Without introduction, I surmise this is his girlfriend.

The fellow on the roof calls to her, and she too goes up the ladder, hauling the bucket.

About ten minutes later they both come down — to my astonishment, without either of them falling.

Of course, with the next heavy rain, water gushes again into our living room from the ceiling, tarred chimney or no. More drastic — that is to say, far more expensive — measures are necessary.

But, after all this, I do realize what I've been doing wrong. I could clearly see what the professionals have been doing that I have neglected.

I need to take up smoking.

Chapter Four

The Morning After

Bill Clinton has made much of his meeting and one and only handshake with President John F. Kennedy. That encounter, when Clinton was but a lad, he would have us believe set him on his course with destiny.

Ha, I say. I can top that: In 1968 I got thrown out of Vice President Hubert Humphrey's hotel room. No, really, it's true.

And as much as I would like to think to the contrary, I do not believe destiny has had anything to do with it, then or since.

As to how I came to be in Humphrey's hotel room in the first place isn't all that straightforward. (That probably doesn't surprise you.)

I mean, it's not as if I'm some sort of politico groupie or anything. Though I have to admit to — ahem — having run into a fair share of big-time national office holders.

I, too, met JFK, though I confess I don't recall that he shook my hand. In fact, I don't remember a great deal at all about the occasion, given as I was, oh, about eight years old at the time. The senator from Massachusetts was running for president and, while driving through heavily Democratic Youngstown, Ohio, in 1960 — in a dimly remembered era before massive entourages and air-tight Secret Service coverage — saw a large group of people milling about outside my school, St. Torquemada of the Bleeding Knuckles, during some function or other.

So on that sunny afternoon, his car stopped, and he got out to mingle and ask for the odd vote or two, no doubt dropping a polite word to the faithful of his own religious affiliation. As an eight-year-old, I pretty much got lost in the crowd. I may not even have managed to touch the hem of his garment. But my uncle Scuppy — yes, yes, that really was his name — long after boasted of a handshake and a slap on the back (though it never was very clear who actually did the slapping, Scuppy or the commander-in-chief-to-be).

Maybe that event started me on my road to politician spotting. A number of years later I made a point to see President Carter and then-Governor Reagan at their respective rallies in Columbus, Ohio, the state capital, during the 1980 campaign — which was hard to do, let me tell you, as their speeches were scheduled for the exact same time, weirdly enough, some four blocks apart. Speaker of the House Tip O'Neill I met also in Columbus, when he stopped in town for a fund raiser and held a leisurely press conference that afternoon.

Richard Nixon, too, was in Columbus for a fund raiser, his for state Republicans. It was his first public appearance of his post-Watergate resurrection. I secured photographer's credentials so I could hear his speech at the soirée that evening.

Members of the press were cordoned off to the side — somewhere to the left and behind the former president's elbow — and were warned to keep behind the rope that separated us from polite society.

Any photos I took that night showed no better than the back of Mr. Nixon's ear. Which I eventually figured out likely was his intent all along.

I caught a glimpse of George Bush the elder at a fête, too, where his wife was introduced by James Rhodes before dinner in the Ohio governor's classic southeastern Ohio accent: "Berbr Booosh hz dip ruts inha." (Translation: "Barbara Bush has deep roots in Ohio." And maybe she has.) And I enjoyed a brief chat with U.S. Senator John Glenn just after his St. Patrick's Day press conference at which he had proclaimed the obvious deadness of his presidential campaign. (The former astronaut found himself short of the green stuff on St. Patrick's Day — get it? Astronaut … the green stuff?)

On the night of Dick Celeste's first gubernatorial election win, I found myself in an elevator with him, riding up to one of his victory parties. (I hadn't worked for his campaign; I was just going to the party for the free drinks and food and, hopefully, to meet undoubtedly ecstatic female campaign workers.)

After a moment or two, Celeste looked at me, nodded and asked, "How's tricks?" Tricks, I thought? Tricks? This from the man about to run one of the five largest states in America? Tricks? So I replied the only way I could think of. "Tricks," I noted, "are for kids."

I was also on an elevator a number of years later, in another office building in downtown Columbus — this time traveling down — when the doors opened to reveal, to my surprise, Senator Bob Dole and about three other men waiting to get on. He must have been in the state capital, I quickly surmised, to shore up some political backing for his presidential bid at the time.

Before I realized what I was doing, I'd pushed the close-door button — mistaken in my belief, I guess, that I had hit the hold-door button — and watched the confusion on the senator's face as the elevator doors closed in front of him. Oops.

~

But I imagine the HHH hotel incident has been the most, well, bizarre case of my political encounters. And it had started out so innocently.

This was in the autumn of 1968, and the local Democratic Party had called my mother to ask if she wanted to volunteer. (We all thought that was rather odd at the time, as my mother has long been a registered Republican. It was probably an omen.) She replied to the caller that she was busy, but told them — she informed me later — that she had a son who apparently had nothing better to do.

I think my mother figured it would be a more productive use of my time than — as she often proclaimed — *Lord knows whatever it was* I spent my days and nights doing then. Hey, I was sixteen. Time management didn't seem all that important.

So the next evening I went along to campaign headquarters, a rented musty one-story ranch house not all that far from our home, without any idea whatsoever about what was entailed or what I would be asked to do.

At first much of what we did, it turned out, involved eating jelly-filled doughnuts from the Amy Joy shop down the street. And listening to two of the party faithful, in attendance almost every night, explain — loudly and to anyone who would listen, even to me — how they had turned up on President Nixon's just-revealed so-called Enemies List.

This was all very shocking — on the *President's Enemies List*. I mean, one of these men even went to my parents' *church*. The other guy I think was a *Republican*.

But our primary function, it was later made clear to me, was to aid the election of the party's U.S. congressional candidate, Virgil Musser, and unseat longtime Representative Frank T. Bow.

Going through the literature we had collected at campaign headquarters, I learned that Mr. Bow, whose perennial slogan was "Frank T. Bow, the Man You Know," appeared in person and in all photographs, buttons and banners wearing his signature oversized red bow tie. Sort of like an old vaudeville comic, along with rubber chicken in one hand, cream pie in the other. I calculated that for this reason alone Frank T. Bow deserved to lose.

Our candidate, Virg Musser, had a slogan so vapid I never was able to retain it in my memory for more than a few nanoseconds. I think it was something as enticing, as invigorating as "Vote for me."

The other basic challenge — beyond this scintillating call for action — was the basic fact that the candidate himself was incapable of showing up for anything on time. And I don't mean he was fifteen minutes or so late. I mean forty-five minutes to an hour late.

We staged one planned spontaneous meet-the-public handshaking opportunity for him at the Boardman Plaza, in front of Kresge's Five and Dime. We'd managed to rally approximately a half-dozen shoppers who not so much wanted to meet Mr. Musser as we kept bribing them with bags of popcorn so they wouldn't leave. (All right, maybe a *few* of them weren't old enough to vote yet. We were going for mass.)

But by the time our congressional hopeful finally showed up — a full sixty minutes late — we'd run out of popcorn and, thus, out of people, too. The only ones left hanging around to shake his hand were the district campaign director, myself and my pal Barty, whom I'd convinced to help. Barty and I had shaken his hand before, but as he didn't seem to remember us, we did it again and called it a successful afternoon.

No wonder this campaign was doomed.

Much of the rest of that fall, in the run-up to Election Day in November, we spent handing out fliers at fish fries, plunking fliers under car windshield wipers at church bingo gatherings and sticking fliers in doorways in various neighborhoods.

We always had lots of fliers, which I found was a good thing one particular afternoon when an exceptionally large and athletic dog took exception to my perceived trespassing on its property and lunged at me as I was about to place a Vote-for-Virg flier in between the screen door and the (what I thought was closed) main door of one home. As the charging beast leaped up for me, huge jaws opening wide to take off my arm or some other body part, I quickly jammed the entire roll of fliers I carried in my other hand down into the center of that gaping mouth of his.

The animal carried on in his trajectory, crashing into the screen door, pushing it and me out onto the front stoop. I went sprawling down the steps to the sidewalk below as Moby-Dick skidded to a stop, completely unharmed and continuing to munch on my entire day's supply of fliers.

I returned to campaign H.Q., assuring our district director that all fliers had been well and truly distributed.

In hindsight, it seems little wonder our candidate had such poor name recognition with voters. Hardly any money was spent on print, radio or television spots. His drive to the U.S. House of Representatives seemed to rely solely on those dopey fliers and on the district director and me riding about in what we deemed the Musser Mobile — I never drove it as I didn't have a license yet — playing a recording over the speaker mounted on the roof that roared *"Vote for Virg, vote for Virg, vote for Virg ...."* I don't believe the announcement actually stated exactly what office this Virg fellow was seeking.

One elderly Hungarian woman I'd managed to chat with on one of my handing-out flier rounds, after much encouragement as to why voting for our man Virg was in her best interests, shook her slender shoulders in bewilderment and asked, "You want me to vote for the Virgin Mary ...?"

As the day of reckoning drew closer, a sense of general panic cemented itself at our campaign center. More fliers were printed, less doughnuts were purchased.

And that is probably why someone there, learning that Vice President Humphrey, caught up in his own demonic campaign barnstorming, would be making a stop at the Voyager Hotel in downtown Youngstown, had the inspiration to send us to the hotel, too, Vote-for-Virg placards in hand.

If the V.P. was going to be there, it was presumed, so would hundreds of national TV cameras. Or certainly a bunch of local ones. All we had to do was get a glimpse of just one of *our* signs on screen, even if only for a moment. That air time would be the coup that would help us bury Frank T. Bow, the Man You Know, and catapult Virgil Musser to Washington, D.C.

It seemed like a foolproof idea. At least, to me it did.

So on the appointed evening, my pal Barty and I, along with Chipper and Ellen — two of the supposedly seasoned campaign experts the national party had sent out to Youngstown to help secure the Congressional seat — made our way to the Voyager Inn. I wore my white styrofoam "Vote for Virg" skimmer (you know, those flat crowned hats with the wide brims only seen of late on young campaign aides — the authentic ones were made of straw and were very popular in early 1900s).

I don't recall if the four of us arrived too early — that seems unlikely, doesn't it? — or if the vice president and his crowd were exceptionally late. But we decided, what the heck, let's go up to his suite and, hey, maybe schmooze a bit with people in the know until the big guy himself arrives.

Again, it seemed like a great idea to me.

Somehow Ellen already knew what room HHH had reserved. So we marched into the hotel lobby, got on the elevator and made our way up — without once being stopped, searched or questioned. All the way up, Chipper — of Connecticut and, he often had noted, of several winning campaigns — kept telling us to let him do the talking.

"I know what to say, so you just let me handle this," he said at about every floor. Fine with us, Barty and I agreed.

The doors opened and we stepped out into the vice president's suite. No vice president, no national media. But lots of Secret Service men. (You could tell they were Secret Service by their special lapel pins, the gin glasses in their hands and by their really ugly brown shoes. And by the guns that suddenly appeared in their other hands.)

"Who," one of the rather angry-looking men asked us, "the hell are you?"

We turned to Chipper. He was going to do all the talking. Chipper said: "Errgg …?"

The next thing we knew we were being escorted, quite literally by the scruffs of our collars, by the Secret Service back into the elevator, down to the first-floor lobby and out into the parking lot.

That left us with plan B: We waited.

A good forty minutes later the limos carrying Humphrey and his group pulled up to the Voyager Inn front doors. And, indeed, TV cameras were there.

We sprang into action. The four of us, each wildly waving four-by-two-foot cardboard Musser placards, raced over to the cars. The Secret Service, seeing us coming, tried to block us from getting too close. But Barty managed to duck around the back of the auto carrying the vice president — we were young and fleet of foot in those days, after all — and just as the man himself was getting up out of the back seat, Barty spun in between Humphrey and one of the TV crew. Barty, smiling crazily, shot up his placard, so what the camera unavoidably would see would be a rather mystified Humphrey with the Musser slogan emblazoned as backdrop behind him.

What happened next, though, was that — in all the jostling — Barty's placard got bumped, or Barty himself got bumped, it all happened pretty fast, and the placard, with Virg Musser's confident face, came down and smacked candidate Humphrey square in the back of the head. WHACK.

The next thing we knew, the four of us were running like insane people down Market Street, putting as much distance between us and the Voyager Inn as quickly as we could.

To our good fortune, the Warner theater, about five blocks away, was showing the just-released *2001: A Space Odyssey*.

The advance word was that the movie was, in the vernacular of the time, mind blowing.

We decided our minds were already blown, and a darkened movie house was as good a place as any to spend the next two hours and nineteen minutes.

It might be unnecessary to mention that Virgil Musser lost in his efforts to oust Frank T. Bow. I don't recall what the final tally was. But let's pretend Mr. Bow's concluding vote count was, say, Jones Beach on Long Island. And Mr. Musser's vote count was one or two infinitesimal grains of sand ….

Or put it another way: Think about it like the battle of Agincourt, and Musser was the French.

I wasn't old enough to vote in 1968, so I couldn't take complete responsibility for the debacle of that campaign.

But somewhere — probably in a box in the basement, I'm certain — I still have my "Vote for me" white styrofoam skimmer. You never know.

Chapter Five

Shoes R Us

For most of the time when I was growing up, my grandmother (on my mother's side) worked as a baker for Strouss Department Store on Federal Street in downtown Youngstown. To visit her, my mother and I would take the elevator up to the seventh floor, then the employees-only elevator to the eighth.

From there, I could find my way back to the bakery with my eyes closed — those tempting smells would pull me past the personnel department, past the executive offices, through what seemed to me as a small child a labyrinth of passageways … until eventually I would enter into the giant expansive of Strouss's bakery. Scores of people — or so it seemed — all dressed in white and with white baker's caps and covered in white flour and white sugar, bustling from counter to counter, from massive ovens to tall wire racks and racks bearing as-fresh-baked-as-you-possibly-could-get wedding cakes and birthday cakes, pies, doughnuts, breads and rolls and cookies and more cookies. And my grandmother would reach over to the racks, pick up one of those flaky, soft and still-warm cookies and gently hand it to me … and she'd say, "There you are."

Upon reflection, it is amazing I didn't explode well before my eighth birthday.

My mother and I often walked the few blocks over to Strouss from the store my father managed. His first duty every morning at Wilson's Shoes, before opening the door for customers, was to take a broom and chase out all the bats. Bats hanging from the shop ceiling, apparently, was considered bad for business.

My mother didn't have a job outside the home in those days, but she would later. She, too, entered into the retail trade and sold shoes for a number of years for one of J.C. Penney's larger stores. And my brother, last I checked, manages a merchandise showroom-type store in Florida.

So, at the tender age of fifteen, when I decided — or maybe my parents decided, in yet another attempt to keep track of my whereabouts — to seek employment, I went to work at a store.

I seem to recall some disinformation on my part about my true age when I applied. But soon I was ripping open packing cases of shoes, arranging and rearranging shoes, ticketing shoes and misleading customers with the best of them.

Over the years, say, from the age of fifteen until well into being a university student, I worked at one store or another. But that first job was at a massive discount store, located in a former warehouse building and tucked alongside railroad tracks and under a railroad trestle, on the far end of downtown Youngstown, not far from the city's oldest strip joint. And it was at that store I was indoctrinated into the ways and means of … truck drivers.

The drivers, see, only had to haul the store's merchandise they were delivering to the very end of their trucks. That is to say, they were not required to bring the stuff onto the freight dock or into the store itself. That, I learned, was my job.

Now the ramp that was to create a bridge of sorts to the edge of the drivers' trucks was this metal sheet-like device that fitted smoothly into the freight dock floor. You first had to pull straight up on this large ring. Then, as you walked backward, the ramp would rise up from the floor, at about an eighty-degree angle. Then you were supposed to walk forward along it, and your weight miraculously would cause the lip at the other end of the ramp to unfold itself. The whole contraption would gently fall back down, forming this bridge, as I said, from the dock to the inside of the truck, and you then could unload the merchandise.

At least, that's the way it was explained to me.

My biggest problem with this whole concept was I then weighed about 120 pounds or so (despite all those cookies in my younger years from Strouss's bakery). I could tug on that heavy ring and — eventually and after much exertion — manage to get the ramp to lift. But no matter what I'd had for breakfast that day, I could not get the damned thing to go back down and connect with the waiting truck.

The drivers, who it seemed were starved for entertainment on those long treks across the country, generally would take a seat on a nearby crate, light a cigarette and guffaw.

It took longer than it probably should have for me to figure out a solution to this almost-daily challenge. I soon had the notion to load up one of our carts with some heavy cases. Then I'd back it up and take a running charge at the angled ramp and … BANG, the combined weight of me and the loaded cart would bring the unfolded ramp crashing down — sometimes to the annoyed surprise of the drivers.

That is likely where I contracted some of the more colorful and evocative phrases of my current vocabulary.

~

As time went along, I got used to the alternating retail pattern of being madly busy then mind-numbingly bored. I soon learned to sleep standing up.

Of course, you really had to keep your eyes open — literally and figuratively — at all times. Shoplifting shoes is slightly different than stealing lots of other kinds of merchandise, after all. You can't just stuff a pair of size-ten-and-a-half brogue wingtips into your pants pockets, can you?

We would have people — people clearly not good at long-term decision making — who would try on a pair of shoes, walk around a bit with them, peer into the floor mirrors — then make a break for the stairs, running as fast as their new shoes could carry them.

Yet I was never certain what my role was supposed to be in this scenario. Was I expected to chase the culprits, knock them down and sit on them until law enforcement officials arrived? ("Great job, Mickey, catching these miscreants single-handed. Here's a hefty raise, and tomorrow we'll hold a swell parade for you down Federal Street.") Run after them, firing at them from our trusty staple gun? Or maybe I should have thrown empty shoe boxes at them, like banana peels in animated cartoons, and hope they slip on one and fall ….

I suspect usually they got away while I was contemplating an appropriate response.

But I must have been doing something right — or not anything terribly wrong — because soon I found myself, with something of a slight bump in pay, at a brand-new store practically out in the suburbs.

So new, in fact, it hadn't opened yet. My cousin Jimmy (I told you retail was in the blood) and I were hired to prepare the shoe department for its grand opening. We assembled the counters and the shoe racks, we unloaded shipments and lugged oversized boxes jam-packed with dozens of packed shoes from the freight dock back to our stockroom. We unloaded those boxes and unpacked the shoes and ticketed those shoes, then put them on the shelves. Then we'd get another big box. And we'd unload *that* box and unpack the shoes and ticket the shoes and put them on the shelves.

This went on for weeks. Believe me, there is no experience quite like pulling pairs and pairs and pairs of dead-weight heavy, slimy, oily fishing boots or waders out of giant cardboard boxes for hours on end. Boots that smell for all the world like … well, like dead fish. Ugly, slimy dead fish.

So when the opportunity came to do something else — oh, please, anything else — Jimmy and I jumped at the chance. Go to the rear of the store, we were ordered, and break down all those cardboard boxes you'll find there and burn them in the furnace.

Now maybe you can imagine how many boxes a new store can collect to be disposed of — all that merchandise came packed in something, and usually it was a cardboard box. Some small, but mostly — as merchandise travels in bulk — pretty darned big.

And back at the rear of the store we found what appeared to be thousands of boxes. An ocean of boxes. Mountains of boxes, some piled haphazardly so high as to almost touch the ceiling.

At first, Jimmy and I would nibble away at the outskirts of this mass of cardboard, taking one box at a time, cutting down its sides with our knives to flatten it, then dragging it out and stuffing it into the furnace. Then we'd select another one and cut *that* up ….

We became bored with this method fairly early on. Soon, it

seemed far more logical and a heck of a lot more fun to race up the side of one of these mountains of cardboard and start flinging down the topmost boxes.

We'd each done this more than a few times when, one time when I was up near the summit, to my surprise — and, yes, in hindsight, I sincerely should have seen this coming — the box I was standing on gave way beneath me. Suddenly I was hurtling downward, crashing through box after box.

I came to stop when I smashed down into the final box, resting on the concrete floor. Every bone in my young and foolish body had been jostled for dear life. But I realized, though very likely bruised, I was essentially unhurt.

Except … except I couldn't move. My arms and legs were pinned to my sides and I could not get out of the box. Because in fact I was within *several* of these packing boxes, as one after another had fallen into the next one down during my rapid descent toward the floor.

I could hear my cousin laughing uproariously as I explained my predicament. It took some time for him to dig his way to my rescue and cut me out. Not because he was unwilling. It just took him a long time to stop laughing.

When opening day finally came, our department, to our surprise, was ready. Shoes were ticketed and all in their places — and I am certain they would if they could — with bright, shiny faces.

It was a fine, warm summer's day and, as we discovered when we arrived that first open-for-business morning, the store's thermostat had stopped working. It was in the eighties outside and, inside, hovered quite a bit above that, even at nine a.m.

And then there was the matter of the sewage pipes. The building itself had been erected at the bottom of a gentle incline. Well, OK, at the bottom of a hill. To save money, the owners had had the sewage pipes run uphill, to the nearest street, rather than routing them downhill to an avenue farther away.

This was a pretty clever idea … as long as the rest rooms didn't get a great deal of use. Not the amount of use, for example, they might undergo when hundreds of customers started coming into the store and using said facilities. I will leave it to your imagination as to what happened next. Suffice it to say, what goes up ….

As the day wore on, it became progressively warmer inside. Customers began to notice. They began to complain. *"What's wrong with this place? Too cheap to run the air-conditioning?"*

One of the owners had an epiphany. He directed one of the clerks to go outside and open up a fire hydrant. They then somehow managed to pump that water onto the roof of the store. The water, he cleverly concluded, would cool off the interior.

The water, however, had other ideas. Its increasing weight, within a matter of thirty minutes or so, became too much for the roof, and gallons of water suddenly came cascading through the ceiling and onto the sales floor, startling unsuspecting customers and sales clerks and seriously ruining racks and display tables of merchandise in the men's clothing department.

Clerks were dispatched to mop up the water, dry off the racks and tables and put out fresh — that is, dry — clothing.

Things probably would have worked out all right after that, had not one of the other owners come into the store that afternoon, decided it was far too hot in there and had an epiphany.

I swear to you I am not making this up.

He directed one of the clerks to go outside and open up a fire hydrant. They then pumped the water up onto the roof of the building, the owner concluding the water would cool off the interior of the store.

And within a matter of only minutes, water began gushing down from the ceiling onto the sales floor, drenching frightened customers and clerks and lots of brand new men's clothing ….

I stayed at that store for a few years. Soon my friend Barty came to work there with me, and we spent our time chatting with the slightly older (that is, more mature) female cashiers and the sales girls over at the cosmetics counter.

In winter, Barty would go out into the parking lot and race around in his Dodge Dart, smashing it into the piled-up snow.

No one ever got hurt, luckily, as just as often as not he performed his one-person demolition derby during store hours.

But, fun though it was, I eventually moved on to a much larger store, one part of a national chain. Things at that establishment were never quite as antic as at the other places — no sudden heavy downpours inside, no cranky truck drivers or automobiles intentionally careening into snow banks, no mountains of boxes to scale. No bats in the belfry, as it were.

On the other hand, my own personal injuries declined significantly. And, who knows, I may even have sold some things. From time to time.

Chapter Six

Tales From the Home Front: Spring
A New Leaf

When it comes to home repair work, I have long considered plumbing the last frontier. That is, on the maps of the Olde World, points beyond which the legends would read: "Here be dragons."

Now I know some of you will argue that doing electrical work is worse. But I disagree. After all, if I mess up with wiring, I'll get electrocuted, I'll die and I won't have to deal with it anymore.

With plumbing, I'm not likely to drown, and there'll still be water everywhere.

It is the same reason God in the Bible chose forty days of flooding, not forty days of lightning.

Now that we've been in our first house for a few years, I have been more than ever convinced of several such beliefs. Another is this: If you can hire someone to do the work for you, do so. It is good for the economy. It is good for your health and well being. It is good for your marriage.

My wife and I have a policy on this. When something major needs to be done — the computer hooked up, book shelves assembled, taxes prepared — the other leaves the premises. For a good, long while, if it can be helped.

Since we've been homeowners, I have added my own silent addendum to that policy: Some home repair work is best done alone, not because the job is difficult and requires loud, foul vocabulary, the sorts of words you don't want your spouse to know you have more-than-passing familiarity with. But because you really don't want her to see how stupidly dangerous some of these things might be.

We've been fortunate. Our house was built in 1923, and it hasn't required many serious projects. A few, but not lots.

Of course, sometimes the simplest tasks have taken on Armageddon-like proportions. I mean, you wouldn't think removing leaves from the gutters would be such a big deal, would you?

First, out comes the ladder. It has to be a tall ladder, so by standing on the next rung beyond the one with the bright red label that says "Do not stand higher than this step" I can just reach into the gutters of the highest point on my house.

Then there is the challenge of actually snaking my hands into the gutters themselves. These gutters, for some reason, are thin, small, bent tubes, with mean-spirited pointy shingles overhanging them, clearly intended to mangle and snag and bloody my fingers.

Yes, I know, don't say it. I do wear gloves. Yes, I tried using a trowel — it didn't fit into the gutters. Yes, I tried using a leaf blower — the leaves were soggy clumps, and when the clever belt-strap harness thing I'd contrived to carry the contraption over my shoulder snapped, I ended up getting royally soaked.

I even tried the notion of firing the garden hose up the drain spout. Even the neighbors got wet that time.

So I reach in, grabbing one handful of glop at a go and fling it to the ground. For a while, I had Lisa stand below to hold the ladder. But she complained of getting filthy, soggy leaves and mud on her. (I don't know why she wouldn't take my advice about wearing one of those green plastic garbage bags over her head for protection.)

~

Once, I climbed up on the roof with the idea of coming at the gutters from above. Take 'em by surprise, if you will.

One morning I waited until Lisa was off somewhere out of the house, then I got up on the garage, then carefully stepped onto the main roof over the back part of the house. I stood up straight, as I'd seen the roof repair guys do, and started walking up to the peak.

Now, at this juncture, I should mention that our house, aside from being tall, has a very steep angle to its roof. The pitch, the roof repair guys called it, when they came out to bid on reshingling. The roof has such a pitch, in fact, the bids all were in the vicinity of what you might pay to send several of your children to college. Ivy league college.

I thought about this pitch theme as I made my way up the roof … and slowly began to slide back down. The morning dew apparently had made the shingles a tad slippery.

I took a few more steps. I slid back, a bit farther down than I'd gone up.

I bent forward, rugby-like, and plowed forward … and slid back even more, this time to the lip of the edge of the roof.

So I sat down to think about this. I looked at the garden down below. And I thought, you know, I'll bet those gutters are just fine. This is a solid house — what are a few more pounds hanging off the sides?

It was time, I realized, to go find something better to do. Work on our taxes, maybe.

Something indoors.

Chapter Seven

Story Problems

Sometimes things just don't add up. It's difficult to believe this now, but when I was in elementary school, I often received an A+ in arithmetic. This was especially remarkable as the school didn't generally award anything above an A.

But mathematics was much simpler then. You had your addition, your subtraction, multiplication and long division, and that was about it. There was an order to numbers, a comforting logic: Ten yellow ducks, take away three yellow ducks leaves you seven yellow ducks.

The problems started when I went to high school, switching school systems in the process. In my freshman algebra class, I came face to face with an evil creation called New Math. No more long division — it was replaced with something sleek and incomprehensible. Story problems that I'd actually enjoyed deciphering in elementary school, like so many detective novels to be unriddled, mysteriously vanished. And my old friend the "x" that had stood for "times" in all those multiplication tables was usurped by a sinister, unblinking "·."

I was traumatized. Math shock. From that moment on, I could no longer calculate the simplest sums. Adding six plus seven required the use of more fingers than I had to spare. Division and multiplication mandated a piece of paper, a pencil and ten minutes, at minimum. I was, in short, baffled by math.

Or, maybe math hadn't become more complicated. Maybe it was the world as a whole. I mean, when I went to work at the bank — for a career of nine long, long months — even taking into account my poleaxed math skills, things were pretty darned weird.

The reason I went to work at a bank was because I'd spent a couple quarters in graduate school and was fairly broke. I needed a real job, one that paid anything higher than what I was earning as a grad assistant — which was significantly close to nothing.

Moreover, I wasn't precisely accomplishing anything staying in school. Studying comma faults in *Pudd'nhead Wilson* was hardly preparing me for a glorious future, in or out of academia. (I'd prepared a paper comparing the humor of Mark Twain and Groucho Marx, but I don't think I was fooling anyone. The only thing that saved my grade that quarter was my professor fell down a flight of stairs at a staff Christmas party and he never got around to reading our papers before the end of term.)

So I'd spent most of those two quarters dating a woman who got out of paying her tab at restaurants by setting the tablecloths on fire … and hanging out at the campus newspaper office.

As I'd officially graduated, there wasn't a position for me there on the paper. (That is, one that paid any money.) But my time there at *The Jambar* — that's a steel making term, though for the life of me I can't recall what it means — was not all for nothing. I did manage to save our advertising sales manager from getting his legs broken.

One of *The Jambar*'s longtime advertisers was one of the burlesque houses in the area — "burlesque" being the quaint word we still used in the early 1970s for those kinds of places. That establishment's full-time manager (and part-time comic), Joey Pickles, was bringing in — for two nights only — Miss Nude Galaxy, and he was firmly convinced *The Jambar* should write a news story about it, he told Allan, our sales manager. Spread the word, as it were, to potential customers on campus.

In fact, he was insistent. Very insistent. He had business associates, as such businesses often did in those days and in those sorts of towns, and they were very insistent, too, Joey implied.

The sales manager and the editor were in a quandary. As with all good publications, *The Jambar* did not write puff pieces on advertisers. And certainly not about strippers, even award-winning ones. On the other hand even a student newspaper couldn't afford to antagonize an advertiser.

And, our sales manager pointed out, there was the not inconsequential matter of Joey Pickles's friends and our sales manager's all-around physical well being. Real or imagined, there was cause for concern on both counts.

The solution, however, came to me as certain as did the

answers to those old story problems from elementary school days. Don't write a news story, I advised my friends. Instead, just as I used to write a movie review column for *The Jambar* back when I was an undergrad and occasional editor, I'll pop around to Miss Kitty's press conference — for, yes, Miss Kitty indeed was her name — and write a *review* of the event. Joey Pickles and his pals will get publicity in the campus paper, Allan will remain bipedal. Everyone will be happy.

The press conference itself, in a suite in a nearby motel, offered free drinks, some finger food, a press packet. The usual stuff. Except for the person being interviewed being completely naked, it was pretty much your standard press conference.

The local TV news crews shot a lot more footage than you'd expect to see on the evening news (and, as it turned out, a lot more than they actually showed). So we ate the free food and drank the free drinks and Miss Kitty giggled a great deal. (I guess she was chilly maybe.) Then Allan, the editor and I went back to *The Jambar* office, I wrote a quick and — to my mind — rather silly six hundred words on the whole thing and the world was at peace. (My column, which I confess sort of made fun of the event as well as the very notion of Miss Nude Galaxy in the first place, even was included in Miss Kitty's press packet for the remainder of her nationwide tour.)

~

But none of this, as I say, was getting me anywhere. Nor was it helping to pay my rent. I needed a job, a real one. So when a friend (indeed, the same one who set fire to restaurant tablecloths) told me she'd heard one of the banks in town was hiring, I showed up at its headquarters downtown the next day and was hired on the spot. (The math test was easier than you'd suspect.)

I reported for duty early the following Monday at the designated branch office, in nearby Struthers, which was built around 1920 and situated between two heavily used railroad tracks and almost smack next to the main gate of one of the then-bustling steel plants.

Now you have to realize that, in 1975, this was before computers revolutionized the banking industry. We tellers balanced accounts with hand-levered adding machines, the kind that made that reassuring *cla-clacking* sound as you pulled down the lever. And when customers deposited funds into or withdrew funds from their savings accounts, we would mark that amount — in pencil, mind you — in a giant book that sat on a counter behind the tellers' cages. Each evening after the bank closed, the book would be schlepped downtown to the main office, where all the information would be entered into the master books. And the next morning, the book would be brought back to our branch office to start anew.

So I tried to settle into a routine, I wore a necktie, once a week I checked the cardboard we'd wedged into the window panes to prevent the glass from rattling when trucks rumbled past and, to my ongoing astonishment, managed to balance my daily transactions just about every night. (If you could not balance your window, you stayed there until you could. And if, say, you discovered that somehow you'd given out too much cash to a customer, you the teller had to go to the customer's home and ask for the money back. I'm not kidding.)

For most of the time, life at the bank was extremely quiet. Legend has it this particular bank had been robbed only once, back in the 1950s: The manager was carrying two sacks of money outside (to give to a Brink's truck? to distribute to children playing out on the sidewalk in some Robin Hood-like act of charity?) when he dropped one of those bags. Passers-by, knowing an opportunity when they saw it, scooped up the cash and ran. Or so the story goes.

Things here generally were still uneventful. Stan, our security guard, who also worked night shift at the nearby steel mill, by midday generally found a comfortable purchase on one of the window ledges and, in the afternoon sun, you could hear him snoring.

Yet, despite my luck in not incurring any shortages — or overages — and the placidness of the job itself, the whole place still was a bit … well, odd. Take Diamanté and Lilly. They owned the bar half a block away, Diamond's. Well, actually, since their divorce, Diamanté owned half the building and Lilly owned the other fifty percent. Lilly owned the half with the living area.

Each Thursday morning, when it would get to be time to send in all the state Lottery money from local retailers and Diamanté hadn't turned up yet with his deposits, I would be delegated to walk over to his bar and peer in through the front windows in hopes of rousting him. And there he'd usually be, asleep on the pool table.

There were the old men who came in every single day to break their large denomination bills for change for their nightly poker games. There was the weary-looking guy who hung around the lobby, wearing his beat up gray trench coat and with a rolled up yellowing newspaper stuffed in his pocket, but who never spoke to anyone, never wanted a transaction — I don't know if he even had an account at the bank.

There was the woman who parked herself in a corner of the lobby and communicated with an unknown higher power by speaking into her left shoe. (Never the right shoe, always the left.)

This particular bank branch office had an inordinately large number of senior citizens (along with an inordinately large number of kooks, apparently). Which was OK, of course, except this was a demographic not exactly trusting of financial institutions. They wanted their money and they wanted to be able to *see* it. When bringing in a Social Security check, for example, each of these sixty-five-plus customers would want the check cashed first, and they wanted you to count the money in front of them. In small denominations.

Then and only then would they inform you they also wanted to deposit, say, forty-five dollars into their savings account. After you'd filled out the paperwork for that transaction, they then would mention, oh, yeah, they also desired to put twenty-two dollars and fourteen cents into their *checking* account.

When we'd finished, I'd explain how it all would be much more efficient — and easier for me — if they would tell me all this to begin with, and likely would reduce the number of errors I might make and generally speed up the entire process. They'd nod, agree that all made good sense. And then, a month later, they'd all come back in and do the exact same thing all over again. Aaarrghh ….

One morning, after a fire at a thrift shop down the street — a fire of no more suspicious origin than any other in metropolitan Youngstown, Ohio, in those days — we arrived at work to discover there was no electricity. The conflagration apparently had burned through some underground utility cables.

This wasn't so much of a challenge as our adding machines, you recall, were hand operated, and the vault opened with a simple spin combination. But without power, that did mean we were deprived of something that was kind of important: Light.

As fate would have it, and often does, that day was not only Social Security check day — the day once a month when we were deluged with senior citizens wanting to cash their checks — but also it was every-other Thursday: That is, pay day at the steel mill. The day when the mill rats, as they called themselves, brought in whopping checks for which they mostly wanted cash — it would not be remarkable for a single teller to pass out in the neighborhood of $32,000 on one of those mill pay days.

Therefore there was lots of counting of bills by flashlight. Even in 1975, U.S. currency was not printed in Braille.

It was, as you might imagine, a hellish day. The mill rats, for their part, thought it was all great fun, and more than one offered to guard the vault. (We thought that was funny, too. But we didn't take them up on it.)

Also turning up that morning was the local parish priest, impatiently hoping to deposit last night's sizable bingo proceeds.

One of my elderly regulars, Mr. Wolzenietski, arrived at my cage right after the doors first opened and refused to leave until he could see each and every one of the dollar bills from his Social Security check payment counted out in front of him. *Ten, twenty, thirty, forty, fifty ....*

Somewhere around early afternoon, the power lines were repaired and the lights snapped on, to rambunctious cheering and applause. Mr. Wolzenietski was still there — *one hundred forty-one, one hundred forty-two ....*

So, as I say, I tried to develop a routine. I brought in paperbacks to read at my window when we weren't busy, which was twenty-seven days out of the month. At lunchtime I took a nap upstairs in the lunchroom. And, as my apartment was in the next county, some forty-five minutes away, I evolved a routine of making a number of stops on the way home at night — at the newsstand for a newspaper, at a bar owned by one of the bank's customers, at another bar owned by another bank customer …. Well, you can see the pattern. In hindsight, it all sort of adds up.

By the following autumn, I'd moved on to a different job and a different career. One that didn't involve math as much. Because, see, whether you're using New Math or old, one plus one, in my mind, still adds up to … wait, wait, don't rush me.

Chapter Eight

Tales From the Homes Front: Summer We're So Vain

If I were going to spend somewhere between $12 million to $20 million for slightly more than a week in outer space, I don't think I would play the Beatles.

It was, of course, California executive Dennis Tito's money, and he could spend his millions however he saw fit. And, that early summer in 2001, he wanted to hang out with the Russians on their 10-day milk run to the International Space Station and listen, he said, to CDs of opera and the Fab Four.

The Russian government, for its part, was quite happy to have someone chip in for the expense — sort of like sharing very, very expensive cab fare.

Don't get me wrong — I like the Beatles, and I certainly enjoy opera (well, some opera more than others).

But if given such an opportunity to listen to music in space, I'd take Carly Simon. Most of her music — about childhood and love of parents, about romantic love and love of adventure — is real and idiosyncratic. *"If all our flights are grounded/Libby, we'll go to Paris ...."*

I like her even if it *is* true she was inspired to write "Anticipation," as she says, while waiting for a date with Cat Stevens.

When Carly did her mini-tour in March 1995 — to get over her stage fright, in hopes of a larger tour later — and it was announced she would perform at a small club about two miles from my home in Columbus, I made every effort to be there.

I got to the ticket-selling outlet hours early.

I waited in line.

And the tickets sold out in the blink of an eye.

I remember standing in front of the cash register stupefied, my now-impotent money wilting in my hand, as the clerk kept repeating, "Anyone waiting in line for tickets to the bluegrass festival ...?"

So, faced with the unthinkable, I found a scalper in the newspaper classifieds and called him to order a pair of tickets for what I can only describe as a whopping amount of money. (No, I'm not telling.)

I drove to his house and, when the scalper handed me my tickets, he smiled and noted that I was getting a good price. After all, he said as he carefully counted my cash, he wasn't a crook or anything.

I've been thinking about Carly Simon more these days because of the trouble I've gone through to hear her. My wife gave me as a birthday present one of those CD players you plug into your car cigarette lighter.

The first day, I actually read the instructions, then turned on the car radio, plugged the big, bulbous thing into the cigarette lighter outlet below the dashboard, slid the cartridge into the tape player, turned on the CD player on the seat beside me … and almost lost a couple degrees off my hearing range.

Once I turned down the volume, it was a perfect world. Carly sang, I rolled down the windows and drove. *"It's the stuff that dreams are ma-ade of …."*

On the second day, the bulbous plug-in thing wouldn't fit into the lighter.

Now, I've admitted publicly and more than once that electronics is not my area of expertise. I looked at the bulbous plug-in thing. I examined the cigarette lighter outlet. Yep, they were both still there ….

I determined maybe the sheath of the cigarette lighter itself had got stuck inside the lighter outlet. So I got out my flat-nosed pliers — stop me if this gets too technical — grabbed onto the lip of the cigarette lighter outlet and pulled ….

This story pretty much goes downhill from here. I discovered no sheath stuck in the outlet, and I managed to push all the wiring, tubing and stuff back in, after a fashion. About two days later, I turned on the radio, wedged in the bulbous plug-in thing and — FRAZZAPPP — a whole bunch of electrically related items on my car suddenly and definitely ceased to function.

Since then, everything has been replaced and all works well. (I wonder if Dennis Tito had this much trouble with John, Paul, George and Ringo.)

But music is very personal, after all. My parents declined to give my brother and me middle names, so sometime in the 1970s I selected mine from a song.

Usually at this point in the conversation, someone says, Oh, yeah …. And starts softly moving his or her head to the music heard between the ears.

But it isn't from a Carly Simon song. I hope she doesn't mind.

I mean, after all, *I* managed to get over *her* marrying James Taylor ….

Chapter Nine

I Got the Call

It probably was about eight or so in the evening, and I'd been working late at the magazine office trying to repair a phenomenally overly long manuscript submitted by one of our freelance writers on exploding radial tires or death row inmates or some equally cheery topic. Before going home, I was making my way to the restroom, which was situated in an alcove in the hallway that joined our offices at *Ohio Magazine* with the main building that housed Larry Flynt's pride and joy, *Hustler* magazine.

(Yes, that Larry Flynt. More about him later.)

As I rounded the corner, I could see the restroom door was ajar and the light was on. I figured someone had just neglected to turn it off.

I pulled open the door and started to enter when I realized the room was occupied. Standing inside, with one foot propped up on the toilet, was a young woman of, I'd say, about average height and very blond hair. She was smoking a cigarette and was wearing ruby red high heels.

And absolutely nothing else.

Damn, I thought to myself as I experienced one of those frozen-moment-in-time moments, I'll bet this sort of thing doesn't happen at *The Wall Street Journal*.

Maybe all newspapers and magazines possess a certain out-of-kilter-ness to them. Or maybe I just can pick 'em. Because it surely has seemed a chunk of my career, my calling, if you will, in journalism has been fraught — yes, fraught — with zaniness.

Zany not so much as in *WKRP in Cincinnati*. More like *Twin Peaks*.

The tiny daily newspaper I worked on right out of university, for example, *The Niles Daily Times* — or rather, *The Daily Times* of Niles, as I constantly was being corrected by long-timer staffers (not that it matters as the publication is defunct now anyway, so I can call it whatever I like).

Staffing and budget both were very small there. So, for our television listings, the receptionist would go out and buy *TV Guide* once a week at the drug store around the corner, bring it back to her desk in our snug little office, then copy (a much nicer word than plagiarize, don't you think?) each day's listings for our own TV schedule.

The weather and, yes, even the hourly news broadcasts on the radio station owned by the same company followed a similar pattern of ingenuity — our news came on 10 minutes past each hour. So our news director had time to listen to larger area radio stations' news reports aired on the hour, jot down a few highlights, then read them on our news segment.

That news director essentially was the entire radio news staff. I would add some news snippets on occasion, invariably from a telephone booth, after attending a riveting school board meeting or a rousing township council session where proposals were discussed for snow plows. *"And this is Michael Chevy Castranova, live from Coal Lump Junction Township council chambers, where bids were taken up this afternoon for this year's new allotment of drainage pipes ...."*

Very exciting stuff.

The Niles Daily Times also was the place where, on about my second or third day on the job, I was told that, as I was going out to interview the county commissioner or wander around an auto assembly plant in the northern part of the county anyway, I might as well take some photos there, too. (Why send two people when one could do both jobs, right?)

And even though I protested I'd never actually taken a picture ever before in my life, a battered Nikkon SLR camera and two rolls of film were plopped into my untrained hands. (I'd actually *won* a photo contest, as the subject, when I was about five or six — in the congeniality category, believe it or not — but I didn't think that's the kind of photo experience the newspaper had in mind.)

That was how I learned how to take photographs.

So every day I would drive out — notepad and camera in hand — to some thrilling trustees meeting or to interview some poor retired steel mill worker in the next town as to why he'd used the wrong amount of sand or salt, or whatever it was he was supposed to use in the sidewalk in front of his house, or to the General Motors Lordstown Assembly plant where the union was engaged in yet another of its long, tedious strikes.

In fact, I'd once taken some great — I mean truly, definitely cool — photos of fractious Lordstown strikers flinging themselves onto the hood of a Lordstown executive's shiny black Cadillac as he tried to pull into the plant through the main gate. Pulitzer Prize-winning stuff, I was positive, as I dashed back to the newspaper office. I was excitedly explaining to the rest of our staff about these undoubtedly sensational shots as I popped open the back of the camera to remove the film ... only to realize, with a sickening sensation around the base of my throat, somewhere near the tonsils, that I'd neglected to rewind the film first.

(My other memorable experience with the Lordstown union was when the head of the local said he'd been informed I had misquoted him in one of my news stories. He hadn't read the article in question himself, mind you, but he'd been told .... He may have been kidding. But I made certain to check under the hood of my car each and every time after that before turning the ignition.)

As for the rest of our staff at *The Niles Daily Times*, there were not, as you'd imagine, very many of us, in an operation that believed most strongly in doing less with less. There was the reporter who covered the city itself — the cop house, the fire station, local merchants, that sort of thing. I got to handle that beat when he was on vacation.

Another reporter really had all her days taken up with editing one of the suburban weeklies also owned by the same company. And that left me to pretty much cover the rest of the planet. Which mostly meant to-ing and fro-ing to village, township and county sessions on farm implements and snow plows. (See above.)

Did I neglect to talk about our city editor? His job entailed yelling at us... and writing about revivals. You know — come-to-Jesus-in-a-tent hooplas, generally held on the outskirts of the county and always emceed by a traveling evangelist. Our city editor only wrote about revivals, nothing else — that was the extent of his beat.

That, and making certain *The Niles Daily Times* front page every day was graced with a photo of an animal. Any kind of animal, and not just from Niles, either. Dog at play in an open fire hydrant in New York City, kittens asleep in a hammock in Iowa City, tarantulas out West doing, well, whatever tarantulas did out West …. As long as it was an animal.

My tenure at *The Niles Daily Times* didn't last terribly long. All that driving to evening council sessions and all that talk about snow plows and salt trucks were more taxing than you may think. Or maybe it was the tarantulas.

Nixon resigned that summer. So did I.

Of course, I since have held down other — many other — journalism type occupations. I'm nothing if not flexible. For a while I even wrote press releases for Victoria's Secret. No, really.

The Les Wexner empire is based just outside Columbus, Ohio, and Vickie's was, and still is, one of his playthings. A friend of mine was, and still is, head of public relations or some equally fabulous job there, and after I ran into her at a restaurant one night, she asked me if I'd be available to do some freelance writing for her. She'd pay well, she said, but the work I wrote for her would have to be done quickly.

So, in a short space of time, I wrote press releases for the changeovers the Victoria's Secrets stores were undergoing then — from sort of reddish Victorian affairs to rather tarty pinkish … um, establishments — as well as releases for a number of products: bath lotions I had never felt, fragrances I had never smelled.

Monica once described writing this way: "You writers are all the same: You sit around and think about things for a long time, then you blow it all out in a matter of minutes." I probably would have been insulted by that if she hadn't been right.

At first Monica was dissatisfied with what I wrote. She wanted more adjectives, she decided, more adverbs. I explained to her the difficulties with describing bath lotions, fragrances and the like I'd never actually come in contact with. But she said it didn't matter *what* adjectives and adverbs I used — just as long as they sounded good.

So I bought a paperback Webster's New World Thesaurus and went to town. Bath lotions became *melodious, coterminous* bath lotions, fragrances evolved into *peerless, soporifically transcendent* fragrances .... Monica was happy, I got paid more money than you'd think for such silliness and my wife, who would have killed to write about Victoria's Secret stuff, was very, very jealous.

Who says journalism doesn't have its rewards?

I also made some very quick cash writing a bunch of chapters really, really fast for the administration of then-Governor Dick Celeste. He'd wanted someone to chronicle the perceived lasting accomplishments of his eight years heading Ohio's top office. I had applied for the job as editor of that project some months before, in fact, but when the state bureaucrat doing the hiring said they wanted the whole book completed — all twenty-some chapters — in a matter of twelve weeks or so, before the governor's term of office ended, I said it couldn't be done. Not well, at any rate.

They hired someone else.

Then, not too long after, I heard from a friend elsewhere in the administration that the fellow they had hired as editor of this legacy project was in a bit of a jam. There was no way, he'd discovered, that he was going to finish all twenty-some chapters before Governor Celeste left the State House. (Hmmm, who would have thought ...?)

So I telephoned him, and he and I chatted. He was desperate. He assigned me a pair of chapters he'd farmed out to two other freelance writers from whom he'd never heard back, for some reason. He handed me a video on the state prison system and some brochures on, I seem to recall, the state worker's compensation bureau. He really needed these chapters right away, he said.

So I went home and wrote them that night. I turned them in

the next day. And he assigned me two more chapters. Just don't mention any scandals or any of the possible indictments against any department heads or anything. I went home and wrote those chapters that afternoon ....

I soon learned the faster I wrote these things, the more he'd give me. And the more money I picked up. In the end, I wound up writing quite of few of the chapters.

As it happened, the proposed book honoring the great accomplishments of the glorious Dick Celeste years was never published. The editor did not meet his deadline at the printer, and the incoming (Republican) administration got wind of the project and put a stop to it almost instantaneously. By early January most assuredly, probably right after the swearing-in ceremony while the new governor was driving to his inaugural ball. From his car phone.

I may, in point of fact, have been the only person who actually got paid from that little adventure.

~

But I would have to say my most outrageous experiences in this wacky, topsy-turvy world of journalism came while I was working for Larry Flynt — he of movie and *Hustler* magazine fame — and his attempt at legitimacy. Tumultuous would be a good word to describe those years.

That was where I met the naked blond woman in the restroom. She was waiting while the photographers got the set ready for her photo spread.

Now I need to be clear here: I did not work on any of Mr. Flynt's more notorious publications. *Ohio Magazine*, as was explained to me during my first or second job interview, was to be his claim to honest, above-board journalism. It would run real stories — hard news, features and photos of men and women with all their clothes on — about real people and events in the state of Ohio. For this start-up, he hired honest, working editors and reporters.

And he hired me.

I had been teaching high school journalism and English in

Zanesville, a small town about an hour east of Columbus, and quickly had come to the conclusion I alone would not be able change public education in America for the better. Or even in Zanesville. I wanted to get back to working on publications. And here was this start-up of a magazine, based in the growing state capital, covering all of Ohio.

The woman who interviewed me for a staff position was named Eileen Seraphin. Her name was so much like seraphim I took it as a sign from God himself that I would be hired, and that He thought the whole thing was a good idea.

Eileen asked me if I knew how to take photographs. She wanted to hire an associate editor who could write as well as serve as staff photographer.

Photos? Sure. I took photos all the time at *The Niles Daily Times*.

Right after she called the next week to tell me I got the job at *Ohio Magazine*, I went out and bought a camera.

In the days and years to come while I was there, under various publishers and owners, *Ohio Magazine* went on to win awards and readers. We wrote about the environment and business, the arts, county fairs and out-of-the-way diners, the State House and Ohio newsmakers. We featured John Glenn and Bob Hope, Ulysses S. Grant and Clark Gable, the Wright Brothers and both Mr. Procter and Mr. Gamble. One news feature I conceived and edited, on transportation of hazardous waste along state highways, was one of five finalists in the National Magazine Awards — the Oscars of the magazine world — within *Ohio Magazine*'s first couple years of existence.

But like rowdy neighbors we couldn't exactly disown, in the early days there were those folk next door at *Hustler*. On more than a few occasions we had to evacuate the entire building — their side *and* ours — because of suspicious (that is, potentially explosive) packages they received in the mail. Setting foot in the main building to locate the vending machines or use the much nicer restrooms often also involved catching a glimpse of staff meetings that included flying furniture. Large furniture, too, not just your small, light-weight table lamps — a whole loveseat once came winging its way out of one editor's office, almost barreling me over with it.

Larry Flynt tried to control the operation over there. (*Ohio Magazine* was pretty much an outpost — almost an afterthought — that he rarely visited.) He'd had cameras installed throughout the main building, presumably so he could keep track of employees via the bank of monitors situated around the massive desk in his office. Generally sleeping under that desk at his feet were his two German shepherds — dogs once seen never forgotten, as they were each about the size and disposition of orcas.

Larry and his wife and second in command, Althea, who'd been a dancer in one of his early nightclubs, ruled his empire by one simple principle, whether that was their intent or not: fear. They spoke, and employees were expected to obey.

The first time I met Larry Flynt — he was dressed in one of his standard far-too-tight T-shirts — he was busy firing someone, and loudly.

One time I was in one of the washrooms in the main building — they were, as I've noted, much better lighted and cleaner than those in our annex — when it was announced over the public address system that anyone in the building having *any* back issues of *Time*, *Newsweek* or, for that matter, *any* other magazine taken out of the company library had better return them to Althea right now. Or else.

As I was watching out the window at that moment, I could see what I first thought was the start of a heavy snow. But I realized in a moment what I was witnessing was not large snow flakes, but dozens and dozens of *Times*, *Newsweeks* and numerous other magazines, pages flapping as they flew downward, being pitched out the windows from the floors above — a blizzard of reading material staffers would rather sacrifice than be found to have in their possession.

And then there was the time Larry bought out one of the granddaddies of alternative newspapers out in California. He wanted to put his own stamp on it, so in the first issue under his reign, he announced, in a giant headline on the front page, that he knew who shot John F. Kennedy.

And he was going to reveal all in the very next issue.

Why wait a whole month to disclose information so shocking

and undoubtedly important to many? Here's a hint: Larry then informed us, the "honest and above-reproach" staff of *Ohio Magazine,* that he had set up a twenty-four-hour hotline, and was publicizing the toll-free number for anyone who had information on the assassination to call in. And we were to answer that hotline.

It became pretty clear to us that Larry probably had no idea who shot JFK. (Why ask people to call in with leads if you already know?) The whole thing was a publicity stunt — one in a long, long series (see: conversion to being born again, etc.) that was intended to boost readership for one or another of his publications.

So, against our better collective judgment, we the "honest and above-reproach" staff of *Ohio Magazine* took turns answering the twenty-four-hour who-shot-JFK phone.

I remember there was a fairly serious blizzard one of those nights, as I skidded along High Street driving to the office downtown to take my turn handling the JFK Bat-phone. And I also recall we did receive lots of calls, at all hours — from sinister men claiming to represent the Cuban CIA, if there is such a thing, and from a woman contending she was Gerald Ford's daughter. (She didn't have any information about the assassination, she just wanted to tell us she thought this call-in thing was a great idea.)

You might not be surprised to learn we never did find out who killed the thirty-fifth president of the United States. (You probably would have read about it somewhere.)

Not long after Larry Flynt himself was shot outside a courthouse in Georgia, some time after the JFK telephone incident, *Ohio Magazine* was sold. We went from receiving our checks signed by the wild, publicity-hungry man who more often than not turned up on the evening news to the other end of the philosophical/political spectrum. The Wolfes, a Columbus family who quietly had made their fortune in shoes, banks, a major daily newspaper and a television and radio station, took over seemingly overnight — we almost got whiplash.

There were some changes in the magazine's content, but not many, not right away. The most significant and immediate event for the staff was our offices were moved. In no time at all, we found ourselves ensconced in the grand old (and Wolfe family-owned) Neil House Hotel, right across from the State House, at the intersection of Broad and High Streets. Beds and dressers were pulled out of one wing of the third floor and our desks, typewriters and drawing tables were pushed in. (Computers were not yet standard issue for publications in those days.)

The hotel-as-office concept was, in a word, great. True, there was the occasional lost and generally drunk conventioneer who'd stagger into one of our rooms and not want to leave. But everyone knew where the Neil House was, it was a landmark. Its lobby had a newsstand, a restaurant and bar; the hotel boasted a parking garage. Our rooms/offices each had their own bathtubs and showers.

But best of all, now that we were in a hotel, was we could get room service. Stuck for a story idea, can't find that illustration we paid $800 for? Relax. Call down for room service.

The Neil House days — even under the solemn ownership of the Wolfe family — were highly entertaining, almost luxurious. But they didn't last, and soon the Wolfes had new digs fixed up for us in space previously occupied by — gasp — an accounting office.

No more bomb scares, no more cigarette-smoking naked models in the restrooms. But no more late-night roast beef sandwiches and bloody Marys delivered from room service, either.

I left *Ohio Magazine* seven and a half years later for a business-to-business start-up that was somewhat less traumatic, at least for a while. No one at *Business First* took off all their clothes during office hours, at least that I recall, and very little heavy furniture was thrown about. There were those trains that roared some scant three yards beyond our floor-to-ceiling windows about a half a dozen times a day, however, rattling not only our telephones and computers but our teeth and nerves as well.

And then there was the time … well, but that was at different publication, and that's another story ….

Chapter Ten
Foreign Correspondents

• *"Camels, on a matter of principle, will kick you. If they are not in a good position to kick you, they will bite you. And if they can't manage that, at the very least they will spit on you."*

— Journal entry, June 7, 1989

If you had asked us then— or, for that matter, at any time for a number of years after, even — what our idea of heaven was, we would have answered without hesitation that it was the bar at the Shepheard Hotel in Cairo.

On our last night there, we gave "Discover Columbus" and "Ohio — The Heart of It All" lapel pins to the two bartenders. They were touched. Everyone in Cairo, as best as we could tell, loved pins, no matter what was printed on them.

We did know the bartenders' names, but among ourselves we affectionately called them Karl and Sasha, after the characters at Rick's Café in *Casablanca*. Sasha was always pleased that he remembered what I drank. This was even though he consistently got it wrong. He'd say, "Whiskey and water, yes?" "Scotch, no water," I'd politely correct him, "7-Up, no ice." Then I'd pour one into the other glass and swill the mixture around, thus avoiding drinking the local water, and Sasha would smile.

The long, dark bar itself wasn't well stocked, and the small lamps placed helter-skelter along it were pretty ratty. But in daytime, diffused light streamed in through the practically floor-to-ceiling windows of the long wall that ran the length of the room. In the evening, the place was sedate and settled, with just an undercurrent of customers' buzzing chatter.

The whole bar area was little more than the entry way to the hotel's huge, impossibly high-ceilinged main dining room, which was under constant renovation — even, we once discovered, at two a.m.

The workmen didn't use power tools, instead chipping out parts of the far wall with hammers and chisels. That way the work was slower and more men could be employed in a city with exorbitant joblessness — and, besides, the hotel probably didn't think it wise to allow the bare-footed guys to use jack-hammers.

In *The Innocents Abroad*, Mark Twain makes some snide remarks about the Shepheard Hotel. But when we were staying there, in late May and into June 1989, in the bar area, whether we sat along the bar railing or at one of its handful of petite tables, it was cool and quiet — except for the almost-constant low racket in the dining room, of course — and our world seemed at peace.

Which on one of those particular evenings was not at all what I would have expected to be feeling. Earlier that day, I had been certain — unswervingly, raise-my-right-hand-up-to-Allah certain — we were not going to live to see another sunset.

That afternoon, we had been on our hands and knees, crawling as fast as we could, following a group of marines dressed in combat gear who were leading us on some serpentine route of their devising into the outer courtyard of the U.S. embassy. A bomb had been reported somewhere in the embassy compound and it definitely was past time for us to leave the premises.

"Sir, sorry for the inconvenience, sir. Sir, keep your head down, sir."

We were going to die, I believed, because it had been foretold by Anubis, the ancient Egyptian funeral ceremonies god. I'd met him the night before, out in the parking lot, next to the opera house, and I was fairly sure that was the message he'd given me.

On the other hand, it was just as likely I'd misunderstood. My ancient-Egyptian-god-to-English translation skills weren't all that honed, I admit. And it wouldn't have been the first time during that stay in Cairo that communications had been, shall we say, less than crystal clear.

When I look back on those weeks I spent there on that working trip, it's all a jumble. I truly cannot recall what happened when … as if all the different things that occurred are like photographs from a long vacation, but all scrambled out of order.

But then, chaos would be a fairly accurate metaphor for the time I spent there. The city and I didn't just have a failure to communicate. I had seemed to have developed some sort of perpetual communications whiplash, careening from one misadventure to another.

I mean, I was there only as a last-minute replacement. I had been sitting in my office back in Columbus, Ohio, minding my own business, just a couple weeks before, when my friend Maureen telephoned to say the other public relations person who was supposed to go with her as part of the ballet company's tour to Cairo couldn't get his visa in order in time and she really needed another person to go with her and they were leaving next week and did I want to go with them? To Cairo?

As I was about to be between jobs, the prospect of some foreign travel — and payment for it, to boot — was too good an opportunity to pass up.

And just about the next thing I knew — after some excessively painful injections for all manner of things and a bit of skirmishing over securing a valid visa in a matter of a few days — I was on an Egypt Air flight bound for north Africa.

• *"The ballet company's interpreter quit today.*

"Very late that night, several of us go to the Cairo Sheraton to watch Oriental dancing — the appropriate name, we are told, for what we call belly-dancing.

"It was not nearly as tacky as we had hoped."

— Journal entry, June 10

During that long nineteen-hour flight to Cairo, I crammed on ballet. I'd purchased a paperback ballet encyclopedia and tried to devour its contents. I also chatted with every member of the group — approximately a score of dancers plus twenty technical crew, administrative types and Ballet Met board members. I inquired about props, costumes and curtains, about movement, theory and inspiration.

I asked the dancers about what and how they danced and why, what they liked about their profession and what they didn't. I found out about their toe shoes (which daily needed repairing) and their feet (which hurt a lot) and what they ate (which was mostly junk food). I learned the correct cognoscente pronunciation of ballet: Not bal-LAY, but BAL-ay — it rhymes with VAL-et and BOM-bay.

Also I had borrowed from a friend an Egyptian Arabic phrase book, in hopes of picking up a few key expressions and not appearing to be a complete dope. When you're in someone else's country, I figured, you're in their home. You are a guest. I wanted very much not to be the Ugly American on Tour.

So I memorized *sho-kren* for thank you, *ay-wa* for yes, *la-ah* for no and *es salæm alekum* for hello.

After we had spent a day or so in Cairo, however, I learned much more appropriate phrases. *Bi-kam dol*, for example, meant how much for these? *Meh-lesh mush-skella* meant no problem, the general response to questions such as, "When will we again see our luggage that was left on the side of the road back at the airport?" And *bo-krah* meant tomorrow, as in the answer to the query, "But you told us that *yesterday*. When will we *really* get our luggage?"

That said, it wasn't completely one-sided. Some of the merchants, and especially the taxi drivers, had incorporated a handful of English phrases into their spiels. Indeed, we couldn't walk past a cab without the driver hailing us with, "Memphis? Saqqara? Giza? You go? I take."

When we would reply we didn't need a cab right now, *sho-kren*, they'd turn to their persistent retail line: "What you want? Gold? Silver? Papyrus?"

Failing that, they'd add: "You want girl?" And, as they wouldn't take *la-ah* for an answer, they'd try: "You want boy?"

But the universal salutation was "Welcome Cairo." At the hotel, in the shops and the bazaars, always a cheery "Welcome Cairo."

That, and "Have a day."

Indeed, relations then between the United States and Egypt were going well, and we found most everyone pretty darned friendly. Well, most everyone.

• *"Robed men with clubs chase after me near Tahrir Square. I'm uncertain what prompted this. As I don't have my Egyptian Arabic phrase book with me, I don't stop to ask for directions."*
— Journal entry, June 3

My primary job in Cairo was to write press releases to fax back to Columbus and other points west and to set up interviews for the dancers with the local media. (None of the computers we brought with us would work once we got there, for some unfathomable reason, so we were lucky Maureen also had the foresight to drag along a good old-fashioned typewriter.)

We were given office space in el Borg — a.k.a., Cairo Tower — the same building where the ballet performed each evening, on Gezira island, just across the Nile from the Shepheard Hotel and a brisk walk across to the other end of Tahrir Bridge. But no citizen of Cairo called it by any of these names. It was newly built on the site of the old Opera House, and "Opera" was what the building still was called. That, or, in honor of the first production to be staged there about a month before us, the Show Boat.

But we weren't in Cairo long before we learned the Egyptian media — through some very different sense of courtesy — apparently thought it rude to ever say the word no.

This was a particular problem when I'd ask a local reporter or TV news producer if he or she could be at the Opera House tomorrow at, say, nine a.m. Yes, was always the reply. And tomorrow at nine a.m. no one would appear.

We weren't being stood up. It's more that they knew in the first place they weren't going to be able to make it at nine — but it would have been impolite to say no.

Once we sleuthed out it was better to ask "*When* would be a good time for you …?," we still weren't guaranteed the interviewers would show up on time — or at all — mind you. But we knew they hadn't gotten the appointed hour wrong, by golly.

• *"Maureen forgets to close the glass windows in our office this afternoon. 'Why bother?' she asks. 'We're four stories up — no one's going to get in to rob us.' She also leaves the lights on. So when we go back that evening after dusk, during the ballet's intermission, we open the door and immediately are pelted by a wall of flying, buzzing insects. They're attracted by the lights and come in through the open windows.*

"In the morning, the entire floor is covered a half-inch-thick carpet of millions of dead bugs. We both consider becoming ill. Eweh …."

— Journal entry, May 29

Years later I was still finding sand in my suitcase. The sand was everywhere in the city. Even carpeting inside the brand new Cairo Tower was doused daily by women carrying water in buckets, to tamp down the encroaching sand from the desert.

There was never a time we forgot we were in the desert. Sometimes we forgot how long we'd been there, and on a couple occasions — mostly in the bar — we even forgot our names. But we always knew *where* we were.

There was the sand and there was the heat. And we were hungry, having been warned to avoid anything grown there or eating any animal that in turn was fed there. (We ate a lot of bread and packaged cookies.) And don't drink the water — we learned to brush our teeth with 7-Up and shower with our mouths tightly closed.

So, when we weren't working or taking up space in the hotel bar, we shopped. Or searched for shopping.

Sometimes those shopping excursions were more of an adventure than we'd anticipated. One afternoon, Maureen and I took a break and made our way to the famous Khan el-Khalili, the massive bazaar where haggling is expected and vendors, if they smile upon you, will escort you to back to their workshops to show how their pots and sculpture and rugs are made.

But … but before we actually found the bazaar we discovered there actually is an Egyptian — that is, non-tourist — side to the Khan el-Khalili, and it is unlike anything we had ever seen. It is dark and crumbling, and its crowded alleys are packed with carts and small cars and motorbikes, goats and — I swear — monkeys.

As we tried to find our way out of the maze of twisting alleys, a small boy attached himself to us. He spoke no English, but continued to talk to us in Arabic, all the time guiding us along, and more than once leading us directly to a dead-end. We'd turn back, and he guided us, eventually, to another cul-de-sac.

Soon, a man was at our side and the boy had disappeared (it was unclear to us if he and the boy had known each other). He spoke English, after a fashion, and he asked after our health and informed us that "Bush is good man," and he asked if Maureen was interested in some very fine carpeting or jewelry. He promised to take us to his brother's workshop, where we could peruse many such wonderful items.

So we followed him, and he led down a few more alleys and then up a flight of rickety stairs built alongside a battered four-story building. (Yes, by this time I was becoming a tad concerned for our welfare. But I thought, hey, it's simply free enterprise and we're here to experience Cairo, right?)

Inside, it took a while for our eyes to become accustomed to the dim lighting. Then we noticed couches about the room, and on them were slouched mostly couples, all of them Western in appearance and dress. Not Americans — we saw hardly any Americans during our entire stay in Cairo — but maybe Germans and Dutch and French, maybe some Brits. They all looked very, very comfortable.

And that's when I noticed the smell. And that's when I concluded we weren't truly being invited up here to view fine carpeting or even jewelry …. Uh-oh.

I reminded Maureen — using as much body language as I could muster — that we needed to return to the Opera House, oh, right about now and we really, sincerely needed to leave. Now.

• *"The Mosque of Mohammed Ali is also known as the Alabaster Mosque, as the entire interior seems to be made of the stuff. Out on the terrace we get a phenomenal view of Cairo. Look — the pyramids on the horizon. And from that spot we hear the chanting prayers of the people of the city, as if in one voice, they rise up to greet us."*

— Journal entry, June 9

On the night before the bomb was found at the embassy and Maureen and I had to crawl our way to safety, we had decided we'd had enough of dance — I mean, geez, how many pas-de-deux can you watch, night after night? — and planned to skip out right after the performance started. Our intent was to scurry to another section of the city, eat in a four-star restaurant (of which the Shepheard Hotel was not, as its main dish was, I think, pigeon) and then seek out one of the city's notorious casinos.

But after I had slipped out of the theater, right after the house lights dimmed, and was scampering through the parking lot to meet Maureen back at the hotel, I noticed a large, all-black dog sitting under one of the alcoves. And I mean large. Fully, in a sitting position, it appeared to me that it would have come up to my chest.

As I looked more carefully, I noticed its ears — long and pointed at the ends. And this dog was staring hard directly at me.

It didn't blink, and I could see its eyes also were black. Then I remembered why this animal looked so familiar. It looked, for all the world, just like the all pictures I'd been seeing of Anubis, the jackal-dog god ….

I dashed to the hotel as quickly as I could, and Maureen and I went about our evening.

But the next afternoon, as we finally crawled out through the last gate at the American embassy, out into the relative freedom of the city, I recalled that … creature, whoever it was, and its staring coal-dark eyes.

And the only the coherent thought that came at that moment to my now much-relieved mind, I swear, was … Welcome Cairo.

Chapter Eleven

Safety First

Heave. Hump. BLAM. Gasp. Heeeaaavve ....

We bought a safe. It weighs 137 pounds, not counting the box it came in.

I'm still not certain why we bought this safe. Maybe because my wife believed our apartment in Columbus soon would go up in flames. Not a bad guess, actually, as we had an electrical outlet that sparked every time we plugged in the toaster oven. Then the fuses would blow.

So we bought a safe. It was advertised as being able to withstand temperatures up to 1,700 degrees Fahrenheit. It was only after we bought it, stuffed it in the back seat of the car, dragged and tipped and rolled it out of the car and through the garage and in the back door that I wondered: What the heck were we going to do with this thing?

What did we own that would require such a degree of protection? Family jewels? No. Priceless manuscripts? Nope. Rare stamps and/or coins? Huh-uh.

Lisa had mentioned storing such mundane incidentals as passports, birth certificates, family photos, that investment stuff our broker keeps mailing us. But in my heart of hearts, my only true valuables were a complete set of Doctor Who trading cards and an early Signet paperback edition of *The Catcher in the Rye* (the one before J.D. Salinger announced he hated its illustrated cover — on which Holden wears that cardinal-red baseball cap turned backward and a matching scarf over one shoulder — and all subsequent versions were the red ones most of us used in high school American lit).

Heave. Hump. BLAM. Gasp. Heeeaaavve ....

We had to decide where to put the thing. What's the point of having a safe for valuables — assuming we would decide what the valuables were, of course — if we just left it sitting out in the open? Wouldn't the burglars go straight for the safe, where the good stuff is? (Notice, by now we had moved beyond fire protection to crime fighting.)

So, as we could determine no way to fit the safe in the first-floor closet, that meant we had to move it upstairs. Up sixteen stairs.

And not wide, spacious stairs, either, but archetypal Clintonville-neighborhood stairs — narrow, shallow, creaky, uneven, splintery wood stairs.

And I obviously couldn't *carry* the damned safe upstairs.

Heave. Hump. BLAM. Gasp. Heeeaaavve ....

When the solution came to me, it seemed simplicity itself. I wouldn't try to lift and actually cart the safe upstairs. No. I would apply the principles I had learned back in elementary school, at St. Torquemada of the Bleeding Knuckles, about pulleys and levers and fulcrums.

I would *roll* the safe up the stairs.

The next day, like a mountaineer about to embark on his ascent, I laid out my supplies — an old pair of my wife's gardening gloves, packing tape and a roll of twine. The need for the gloves was obvious. The tape was to keep the safe's packing box closed. And the twine was to hold the box together as I rolled it upstairs. I chose twine because it was thin enough to slide under the box without having to lift the safe.

My goal, you see, was to never lift that thing again — not that day, not ever.

I taped and twined and shoved and pushed the ponderous package to the bottom of the stairs, denting and toppling only a few hapless pieces of furniture along the way. I surveyed the climb. Piece of cake, I thought.

I shrugged on the gloves, bent my knees as I'd learned to do back when I worked on a freight dock, slipped my fingers under the edge of the box and slowly, calmly, breathing deeply, tilted the box … up, up … when suddenly it took on a life of its own and crashed up and over and down onto the first step with a thunderous CRASH.

I threw my back against it before it toppled back onto the main floor. Whew. The safe didn't seem so heavy resting on the step, but I clearly would have to keep in mind the momentum portion of the physics equation.

That is, I'd have to make sure the safe didn't fall back on me, oh, about midway up the stairs. That, I realized, gazing up at more stairs than I had noticed before, could be an unpleasant experience.

OK, on to Step Two. Deep breath now. One, two, three.

Heeeaaavve. Hump. BLAM. Gasp.

Now Step Three.

The safe, I could swear, was getting heavier. Two hundred pounds now, at least. Don't panic. Tilt … tilt … BAM. *CRASH.*

This was all taking longer than I'd anticipated. About two-thirds of the way up and I was very, very tired. My arms were sore and my fingers numb.

That's when I noticed the cardboard box was coming apart. Yes, the *box* indeed was going up the stairs — but the *safe* itself, the hulking grey beast, was sliding out of the box and *down*.

The only thing between it and its gravitational destiny — literally — was me.

With my right hand on top of the box, my left hand along its side, my head and shoulder against the drooping bottom, I pushed. Eerrrhh ….

Why had we bought it? Were we vain and greedy, trying to hold on to what everyone knows you can't take with you? Had we become middle class?

I tried to think, as I stood contorted on the steps holding up the weight of the world, just whose fault was this anyhow? I wanted someone to blame.

Just then the safe shifted, and not in a positive direction. I considered letting it slide back downstairs and forgetting this whole really bad idea.

But I realized that when it did finish its well-deserved plummet to the bottom, we'd have a smashed front door and most likely a safe lying out in our front yard. Not the best location.

So I began to push again. And slowly, slowly, the safe made its way back onto the step. Then up, up, up, *BAM*, onto the next step.

It took another ten minutes to reach the top of the stairway. I then slid the safe along the hall to the bedroom closet.

My arms hurt. My back hurt. My neck hurt.

Still, I had to admit to a feeling of accomplishment. Man against machine. Lisa undoubtedly would be impressed.

Buying this safe wasn't such a rotten idea after all. We *could* have a fire. We *could* be burglarized. My Doctor Who trading cards and *The Catcher in the Rye* with the cover that J.D. Salinger hates would be safe.

I pushed the safe into the closet, tugging off the remnants of the box. It fit perfectly. A handsome safe.

I tested the handle — locked, secure and tight. Safe at home.

Then I looked around for the combination. The last I saw of it — neatly typed on a tiny piece of white paper — was when I put it inside the safe when it was downstairs ....

Uh-oh.

Chapter Twelve

Tales From the Home Front: Autumn
Green Fingers

And so in the last moment just before my wife gets in the car to leave for her week-and-a-half-long trip — a trip she's known about for a year, mind you — she says to me that it would be a really good idea for me to move some of her plants in her garden while she's gone.

Plants. Garden. Dirt. Mud.

My relationship with plant life and the great outdoors has been fairly well established for years: I don't mess with it, it doesn't mess with me. The outdoors, I've expounded upon more than once, is what you have to go through to get to your car.

So Lisa and I walk around to the side of the house and she points out the two plants in question. House painters are expected any day now, and she would like these two in particular moved out of harm's way, to elsewhere in the garden patch.

She starts by noting that the pair of plants she wants relocated — the names of which are gone from my memory bank nanoseconds after she speaks them — are "leafy." Well, I reply, all the plants are "leafy" — that's why they're plants.

Are you sure, I ask, that isn't poison ivy?

Lisa sighs and steps into the garden, standing next to the first plant, then moves over to the next one. To make certain she hasn't understated her case, she points to them.

OK, OK, I say, I've got it, trying to appear confident.

And that's when she — perhaps inadvertently — dooms the plan to failure: As she is stepping out of the garden, she points out a trio of other plants I should feed to her pet rabbit while she's gone.

We have now gone beyond my information-holding limit — any amount of anything more than three items requires a written list. I nod my head repeatedly and say not a word. Lisa gets in her car and drives off.

I believe what happened next was not entirely my fault.

About a week later, after a few rainless days when it seems that indeed painters actually might show up, I go out to the tool shed. The tool shed is a part of our household I go into twice a year. In spring I pull out the lawn mower and push in the snow blower. In autumn, I reverse the situation.

After rooting around in there for a while, I find a dandy spade — hey, I remember buying this once upon a time. I sling it over my shoulder and march over to the garden, prepared to move if not mountains, certainly a few bits of plant life, as well as take up some leaves for the rabbit's supper.

(The bunny's name, for the record, is Chloe, and he lives in the house with us. Well, actually, we started calling him *Mister* Chloe sometime around his six-month birthday, after certain previously unsuspected discoveries — despite what the veterinarian had told us — were made.)

However, now face to face with all this identical-looking greenery in the garden, I come to a fearsome realization: I have absolutely no idea which plants are supposed to be moved. I have completely forgotten.

I try not to panic. Let's see, she said the plants — were there two or three? — were green. Or they had leaves. Or something.

Trapped, I resolve to be decisive. I step to the back of the garden and dig up the plant closest to the wall, then replant it at the front of the garden. (All right, I dig a hole and slap some of the dirt back alongside it. I was absent on plant-relocation day in high school biology class.)

Then I dig up another one. Then another ….

By the time I've finished, I've replanted maybe a dozen of these miserable green things, large and small. Better safe than sorry, I say.

Concluding a good day's work has been done, I put away the spade and, before going into the house, return to the garden to select some leaves for the bunny. Let's see, the plants he can eat are the ones located right about …. No, no, they used to be the ones right over … ummm ….

Chapter Thirteen

No Small Parts

I was watching an old *Doctor Who* episode on video when Pam telephoned. It was *The Web Planet*, from 1965, the story in which the Doctor, portrayed then by William Hartnell, does battle with men dressed up as giant ants. Great stuff.

Pam was calling to tell me about a general audition this coming Sunday downtown for a movie to be filmed right here in Columbus by a couple young — well, not that young — directors. They were friends of hers, she was running the auditions for them, there was no money to pay actors but it was going to be a super project and there was a great part just ideal for me, she said, almost all in one breath.

This was at the time of my life when I'd pretty much moved beyond the notion I'd have a career as an actor. I'd even moved beyond the idea of having it as a hobby.

True, just like almost everyone else on the planet, I'd always harbored a secret desire to perform. This probably came from a childhood spent in Youngstown, Ohio, where, with the aid of a two-story television antenna affixed to our one-story ranch house, we were able to pick up twenty-four-hour stations from Pittsburgh and Cleveland. On nights when there was no school the next day, I was permitted to stay up and watch television until dawn. And watch I did, just about the only thing broadcast late at night in those days: movies. Musicals, gangsters, cowboys, comedies and dramas … all from the 1930s, '40s and early '50s.

(Quick, off the top of your head: Can you name your top six favorite movies? I can. In no particular order they are *Casablanca, The Seven Samurai, Citizen Kane, Some Like It Hot, The Bicycle Thief* and *The 400 Blows*. Notice they are all in black-and-white.)

This hankering to perform — psychologists only later would

call it acting out — started early. In Cub Scouts, when I was, oh, eight years old, maybe, my den put on a play, the plot of which is long gone from my memory. But I do remember being on that small wooden stage, alone, and that I was supposed to say my line — "I shot an arrow into the air," or some such — and fire this plastic arrow from my tiny bow. Except that I fumbled the arrow and it flopped to the stage. I picked it up and tried to draw it back on the bow, but I kept missing the bowstring. People in the audience started chuckling. So I kept fooling about with my little bow and arrow, dropping it, being unable to find it on the floor, having it fly up over my shoulder. And the audience laughed even more.

At one point I even ad-libbed something like, "That's what I get for buying wholesale."

Our den mother was furious as I had strayed so far from our rehearsed timetable, but I was delighted. It was as if I'd found my long-lost home. Broadway couldn't be far from that little church social hall stage.

In reality, however, it was a number of years before I got on a stage again as a performer. Thirty-three, in fact. Lisa — who was not yet my wife — and I both were asked by the woman from whom we were taking some acting classes to be in a production she was staging of a play I think was called *Beheaded*, or *Doomed and Despondent* or something like that. It allegedly was comedy.

Lisa and I were definitely low on the company pole. Just about everyone else in the cast had been doing this sort of thing for years around town. So it fell to us to handle props, move furniture and each play more than a few parts.

I had met Aïda through an improvisation group she ran. (Improv was better than traditional stage acting, I'd decided — there weren't any lines to learn.) She had even offered me a contract once. I calculated I'd make about $600 a year, so, flattered though I was, I told her I'd have to think about it, for a really long time.

Aïda, of course, was not her real name. But it suited her, given her operatic nature. And *Doomed and Despondent*, we learned later, was a play Aïda had staged before — several times, in fact — at various locations throughout America. And each time, she had cast herself in the female lead, as Rachel, a neurotic character who may or may not have poisoned her husband and was on the lam. Did I mention this play was a comedy? I'm not certain anyone in the audience ever figured that out, either. Most nights ended up with several audience members in tears, sobbing for poor Rachel.

But I have to say Aïda, as our director, was determined and extremely skilled. It was, after all, her parent's money they'd given her for law school she was spending to stage this particular play, so she clearly knew her stuff.

She was a gifted actor, was very knowledgeable about her trade — she had done episodes of *911* or *America's Most Wanted*, and knew about emotion, make-up, about blocking and lighting … and therefore we were all extremely afraid of her.

Aïda's Columbus production of *Doomed and Despondent* saw six performances, and I believe it would be fair to say something went bizarrely wrong each time. One night the actor who was playing Tom Jr., who, while wearing a ski mask, was to sneak around the side of the audience's seats, then jump out with a gun and shoot Rachel, forgot to put on the ski mask. Everyone could see who he was. Another night he forgot the gun. That made his shooting of Rachel rather unconvincing.

And one evening, the actor playing Lloyd, while dressed as Santa Claus, gestured a bit too expansively and smacked his arm into the four-foot-tall Christmas tree on stage, sending it arcing into the audience. (There were only minor injuries to the people hit by flying ornaments and hot lights. The tree itself, however, did not survive the incident.)

But my favorite surreal happening was the evening a pair of American Sign interpreters had been hired to sign for some hearing-impaired folk who'd been given complimentary tickets for that performance. (See, the play also has a character who pretends to be hearing-impaired to romantically attract one of the possible murderers. No, it doesn't seem all that amusing to me, either. I could, on the other hand, be missing something.)

But the bus bringing the hearing-impaired audience members to the theater broke down, so they never actually arrived. The signers, however, carried on, and there they were all throughout the entire performance, moving their hands and interpreting the play to a huge section of dark and empty seats.

Pam had been in that cast of *Doomed and Despondent* — with a deservedly much larger part than mine — and now, not too many months later, she thought there was just the part for me in this local movie.

So Sunday afternoon I went along to the auditions for *Moon Goats on Mars*. What I read of the script while waiting my turn seemed to be about science fiction, but we had been told, more than once, no, it was not about science fiction. It was about alternate reality. Oh.

I never did determine what the title *Moon Goats on Mars* meant.

The character Pam said I should read for was described in the notes, to my surprise, as a troglodyte. Now, I've never claimed I was Cary Grant, or even Ulysses S. Grant, but I didn't really perceive my stage career as essaying the role of a cave dweller.

But I did the reading, remembering to smile. (That was one of those acting tricks I'd read in an Uta Hagen book or somewhere — play against type. You know, if it's an angry character, whisper. If it's a cave-dwelling troglodyte, look happy.)

I wasn't actually offended when I didn't get cast in the part of the troglodyte.

I did, however, land the role of Stimjoint Virtual Reality User (remember: not science fiction, but alternate reality), and happily showed up a few Sundays later at the warehouse where much of *Moon Goats on Mars* was being shot. Where, to my confusion, I was directed not to costuming or make-up, but to special effects.

My costume, it seemed, involved my being fitted into this barber's chair, with massive gloves on my hands and heavy wiring up and down my arms. And over my head was placed what once was a football helmet but now bore wires and plugs and a handful of flashing lights.

The first problem, as I explained at the time to Tim, the special effects coordinator, was that the football helmet/stim suit nodule/whatever-the-hell it was, was too small. So Tim climbed up on a ladder to get above me, as I was strapped in the barber/stim suit chair, and pushed the helmet straight down onto my head, almost removing one of my ears in the process.

The other problems, I discovered in rapid succession, were that the helmet/stim suit nodule was very, very hot, especially under those camera lights, and that Tim the special effects coordinator seemed to forget I was strapped into the chair and couldn't get out without help. So when breaks were called, the crew would wander off for a cigarette, make some telephone calls, rehearse their lines, talk to the directors … and I would be trapped in the barber/stim suit chair, one of those light bulbs in particular getting progressively warmer somewhere around the back of my neck. "Tim? Tim? Hey, someone … anyone?"

Nonetheless, when the camera was on me, I tried to acquit myself with all that I had learned about this noble profession called acting. I had no lines, I was to move about as if I were being … well, stimulated, I guess. But I sought my motivation. I remained centered in my character of Stimjoint Virtual Reality User. I stayed in the moment, in the now.

It was, except for the scorch mark on the back of my neck by early afternoon, a good day.

Probably a full year later I received an invitation to the premiere screening and reception for the finished movie, now called for some reason *The Greater Gorgonzola*. (Or something very much like that.)

At the reception the directors and the writer, dressed in tuxes, gave generous speeches. The female lead, in her gown, waved. The male lead didn't show up as he was doing television commercials, we were told, in Los Angeles. Oooo ….

Then the auditorium lights went down, and we watched the movie we had labored over for months. Well, OK, I personally labored over it only about a half day, but I was committed to the vision.

And the movie was … really bad. I mean, the acting, lighting and sets were somewhat convincing. But after all was said and done and the lights in the auditorium came up, I still had no bloody idea what this movie was about.

And my part as Stimsuit Virtual Reality User lasted, all told, about eight seconds.

After the reception — where I had scarfed up as many of the little chocolate-dipped strawberries as I could carry — we went home and I put in a *Doctor Who* video, this one from 1975, *The Claws of Axos*. In this adventure, the Doctor, now portrayed by Jon Pertwee, does battle with men dressed up as what appeared to be giant clumps of seaweed.

As fine acting as you'll ever want to see.

Chapter Fourteen

The Frog and I

My wife is from Louisiana. I say this not as an apology, though sometimes people think it sounds that way. I mean it more of a way of explaining that she and I had remarkably different upbringings and, therefore, now have widely divergent views on some matters. Different, if not necessarily opposing, world views.

This is significant because — as part of our pre-nuptial agreement — I consented to go with Lisa once a year to visit her family in north central Louisiana.

Where her parents live — and where my wife grew up — is in the woods. Not *near* the woods. *In* the woods. In a location so remote there really isn't a town there. Mail is addressed to Goldonna, about a half an hour away. In fact, only in recent years was the dirt road near their house given a name — the post office named it after my father-in-law, so it is called A. Williams Road.

A culture in such, well, isolation has developed what an outsider (that is, me) might perceive as, well, quirks. Their names, for example.

I have tried on more than one occasion to convey to my wife why someone named Mr. Pet is funny. Not that Mr. Pet *himself* deserves to be considered a subject of mirth — why *calling* someone Mr. Pet is funny. Or his wife, Miss Violet.

The last time we had this conversation, Lisa was describing a branch of her family tree, upon which hung a variety of folk, some of whom were related and some who were not. (Mister and Miz and Uncle and Aunt are titles applied, apparently, regardless of actual blood or contractual relationship.)

The Jones family, she noted, had five children — three girls and two boys — only three of which she actually can remember the names of. One of the anonymous sisters was married to Mr. Otis, about whom all that's remembered is that he worked for the fish and wildlife service for a long time. Another sister, Miz Faye (but not, for some reason, Aunt Faye, though I don't know why) married a man named Odell (that would be his first name, mind you), and they had a daughter, Barbara Lou.

Both Barbara Lou and her husband, Jimmy Dale (nope, Dale is not his last name), were both school bus drivers. Jimmy Dale was, Lisa said, "from somewhere else." Somewhere other than Louisiana? No, she replied, somewhere other than Winn Parish.

Barbara Lou and Jimmy Dale had a son they named Mickey Dale.

Miz Faye had two other sisters, Miz Ardell and Miz Maybelle, and a brother, whose name is lost to posterity. That brother had two sons, Charley and Frog. (Frog was so called, Lisa said, "because he was always little …..")

I admit that, usually by this stage of family description, I have lost the trail and don't really recall why we began the conversation in the first place.

Trips to the homestead traditionally have varied in degrees of uneventfulness. There is, after all, no newspaper, no TV (the reception is terrible) and the solitary radio station apparently can pick up only Paul Harvey.

The only excitement I truly remember was one evening, during a fairly serious rain storm, their dog had given a sudden yelp from somewhere outside, then was silent. Lisa, her mother and I went out to investigate. There had been renewed reports of — I'm not kidding — a cougar thereabouts, people had heard it wailing, and we were concerned for the dog's safety.

Out at the dog's shed — though lean-to would be a more apt description — we found its chain leash had been snapped, so we determined it had run off after … something.

At this point, standing in the mud and drenched from the rain, in the thunder and lightning, and at the exact same moment as my flashlight died out, I had an epiphany. It went something like this: I concluded that the dog could take care of itself. I also concluded that, if indeed there were a cougar or a jaguar or a whatever the hell it was out here, we most certainly must be out of our minds.

We returned to the house with all deliberate haste, deciding to let nature take its course — just as long as we were not part of it.

My father-in-law on occasion has asked for my help on some project or other around their house or on their subsistence farm. (They often ask if I know where potatoes come from, and I always reply, yes, from the grocery store.)

He seeks my help, I assume, to relieve my boredom, rather than through any misguided notion I have any skill whatsoever with any tool larger than a Post-It Note. (This is the same father-in-law who generally introduces me as his Yankee son-in-law who went to Harvard. I am not certain this is meant as a compliment to my obvious intelligence and Kennedy-esque charm.)

During one visit he asked me to help him sharpen the blades to his lawnmowing tractor. Figuring that all I would have to do would be to hand him whatever tools one would need for such a task while he did the actual work, I said sure, let's have at it. It did not occur to me the blades still would be affixed underneath the tractor itself.

Out in the yard, seeing the situation, I asked how exactly we were going to get to these blades. Audrey came out of his tool shed with a rather short piece of rope and what I took for a winch. His plan was, if we can't get to the blades, we would bring those blades to us.

Audrey put one end of the rope around the low branch of a particularly smallish and rather aged crabapple tree out back by his potato field and asked me to tie it off. He then handed me the other end and suggested I knot that around the bottom of the tractor.

Now this wasn't a large tractor, as these things go — or, at least as I imagine, never having actually been up close before to any kind of tractor, except maybe driving by one, with it out on the side of the road while I whizzed by on the interstate. This model was about the size of a golf cart, but it was bright red, and had a sort of mean look about it.

After asking Audrey about three times if he were absolutely positive the thing was shut off, I laid down and reached under its front axle, where I wrapped the rope around and tied it.

I stood up, and Audrey said, "OK, now winch it up." I looked at this tiny, scrawny tree, then back at the bright red and definitely hefty-looking tractor. There was some basic premise of physics that was escaping us here, I was certain, but I couldn't put my finger on it.

Planting my feet and grabbing the rope, I tugged. And tugged. And tugged some more. Slowly, and without giving so much as an inch willingly, the front end of that damned tractor slowly began to rise. The tree, to my surprise, bent a bit, but remained vertical.

After I had the tractor tilted about two feet up off the ground, my father-in-law decided that was good enough, and disappeared back into his toolshed. After some banging about in there, he returned with what I could only guess was once a really nice pair of pliers. A pair of pliers from maybe a children's toy tool set. I had never seen yellow ones before.

"Here you go," he announced, handing them to me. "Now you have to loosen the bolts."

I have to say, at this stage, I wasn't entirely pleased with the prospects. Audrey, sensing my hesitation, said not to worry, that he would hold onto the rope.

Figuring he wouldn't actually be able to hold onto the tractor, too, if the rope broke, I didn't ask, and got down on the ground. I slithered under the tractor to see what was up. And indeed, there were the blades — big, vicious looking things, covered in dried grass — a pair of them held on by remarkably flimsy appearing wing nuts.

I took a deep breath and latched the pliers onto one of them. I twisted the pliers. Nothing happened. I twisted them again. Not a budge. Well, OK, being quasi-ambidextrous, I have this problem from time to time. I tried twisting the other way. Still nothing.

I applied a little more pressure, at the same time checking out of the corner of my eye to make sure I could see Audrey's feet out there, and hoping he still had his hands on that rope. But the wing nut gave up nothing.

Crawling back out, I asked Audrey if he might happen to have any other pliers. Maybe some that were larger and possibly not made out of yellow plastic by Hasbro. He said, no, no, that was the only one he knew of.

At that stage, noting the slender tree that was holding up the tractor wasn't looking any more robust, I pretty much admitted defeat, saying no more progress was going to be made this day on this chore without a severe upgrade in equipment.

Audrey conceded that was all right, that he would call another son-in-law who lived about an hour away and had his own tools.

Fine, I decided, I'd done my bit. I had at least gotten the bloody tractor up off the ground.

When we left at the end of our stay a couple days later, that bright red tractor was still out there, precariously up on its rear wheels and tethered to the tree. I've had dreams since then, that that tractor is still there, strung up to that tree, waiting. Waiting for me. It and all its relatives — Jimmy Dale and Ardell and Maybelle and Frog. And that it is very, very angry.

Chapter Fifteen
Cotton Club

My father-in-law has put his hands to many chores in the past 76 years of his life.

He tells me when he was a young boy during the Great Depression he picked cotton by hand, in fields not far from where he lives today — in north central Louisiana. He and my wife's mother work their subsistence farm of potatoes and peas and other vegetables not near any main roads with traffic lights, but out in the woods, really.

For most of his adult years Audrey worked for the federal government, marking trees so the timber companies would know whether they legally could be cut.

Timber is still one of the few occupations here in Winn Parish, in some form or another. The Stone Container Company, the major employer, supplies shopping bags to the Wal-Mart in Winnfield and elsewhere in the region. You often can hear the eighteen-wheelers barreling along out on the road, carrying their cut trees to the paper mill.

Tonight my father-in-law, long retired from the tree-marking business, is putting his hands to another chore. Once a week for the past fifteen years or so he climbs into his pickup truck and drives over to the Backwoods Inn.

There he joins anywhere from four to eight other men and women from the community to provide entertainment — he plays the fiddle, many of the men play guitar, one woman sings, another man strums the steel guitar ....

The musicians perform free. Music ranges from Bob Wills and Hank Williams tunes to — once in a while — songs my Yankee ears recognize.

The Backwoods Inn has been under the same ownership since it was built in 1980, some nineteen years ago, by Sybil Womack, who tonight perches near a cash register that separates the dance floor from the dining area.

The inn is spare, a modest-sized room, with long tables in the restaurant section — featuring a salad buffet, cake and coffee — and a mix of chairs (and one well-used couch) more or less circling the dance floor. Admission price to the dance area seems to be whatever you can afford to pay.

~

This Saturday evening, nine male musicians and one female singer crowd the front area of the dance floor, and some two dozen hopeful dancers occupy chairs, waiting.

Many of the patrons are in their 70s and 80s — widder wimmin, as they are called, outnumber the men three-to-one. Except for one notably well-dressed couple — the man is wearing white cowboy boots and a bright red shirt with gold tips on his collars, the woman has matching gold shoes — customers at the inn tonight aren't in couples.

A dance begins with one of the men crossing the dance floor, then stopping — as if to his own surprise — in front of one of the women. The man then does a sort of abbreviated hoedown kind of step, and the woman, face beaming, stands and does a reply hop step — it resembles a mating dance, and it is, in a way. The pair then links arms and moves out onto the floor.

The men rarely last more than one dance before they need to sit down, puffing and sweating heavily — the temperature this spring night is in the 80s, after all, and there is much talk of recent heart surgeries and farm accidents — and the women return to their chairs to wait to be chosen again.

Audrey takes a break — the other musicians are playing songs he says he doesn't know that well — and chats with Sybil. My mother-in-law has been talking in the restaurant area all evening. They'll be here for only a few hours, but it is the social event of the week. The well-dressed dancing couple left — together — about an hour ago. Everyone noticed.

When I tell people we're going to Louisiana, most ask if we'll be sampling any of that great Cajun food. They assume all Louisiana is New Orleans.

But Winn Parish is many hours and many miles from the *laissez les bon temps rouler* of the southern part of the state. This is a place of hard work and simpler pleasures, enjoyment the people who live here have to work for and harvest — just as they work the soil of their land.

It is not difficult to come to this conclusion. Just look at my father-in-law's hands.

Chapter Sixteen
Traveling on Our Stomachs

There are many reasons to go to Paris. It is, of course, the city of writers, and ever since college I wanted to visit the inspirational source of Fitzgerald and Joyce and home of Hemingway's moveable feast.

It is the city captured in evocative black and white in the New Wave movies of Truffaut and Godard — tragic little Antoine dodging down side streets with his stolen typewriter in *The Four Hundred Blows*, sly Jean-Paul Belmondo trying to charm sexy Jean Seberg along les Champs, as he calls it, in *À bout de Souffle* (*Breathless*). For those images, I loved Paris even before I ever went there.

There is the art — more art than you can see in beaucoup journeys to this city. In just one wing alone of one museum, the Louvre, for example, you can find the expansive masterworks of Delacroix's *Liberty Leading the People*, Géricault's *Raft of the Medusa*, Jacques-Louis David's massive (deep breath now) *The Consecration of the Emperor Napoleon and the Coronation of Empress Josephine*.

Good gosh, before capitulation to the euro, the French even printed pastel illustrations of the Little Prince on their *currency*.

The city also boasts neighborhoods of diverse cultural and architectural tastes — the elegant Champs-Elysées, the bohemian Rue Mouffetard market area, the trendy-yet-homey Marais, the cafés along the Boulevard Saint-Germaine ….

There are all these admirable reasons to make a trip to Paris.

But my wife and I mainly go there to shop.

OK, I admit that sounds so … so *déclassé*. But I've gotten a jazzy charge every time we've been in Paris — invariably a matter of weeks before Christmas — and the major department stores, festooned in white and gold, are packed with bustling shoppers, and the display windows of Au Bon Marché, Galeries

Lafayette, Printemps and Samaritaine are animated with jolly blue and red stuffed marionettes acting out cheery holiday pageants — decorating trees and hanging festive lights, baking Christmas dinners, gift-wrapping toys — to entertain the entranced children out on the sidewalks.

Paris is a retail mecca. If you want it, surely you can find it — or probably something much, much better — in this city.

Truth be told, all that shopping also can work up an appetite. And, as my wife, the professional restaurant reviewer and food writer, has said more than once, she sees no point in going somewhere on vacation to have a bad meal.

Virtually every repast we've enjoyed in the so-called City of Lights has been — in a word — excellent. They were wonderful. They were beyond perfection.

Even the dinner we finally were served at one Rumanian restaurant on our most recent visit wasn't actually terrible. It's just that, by the time the food was placed in front of us, I admit I was in a pretty *enfant terrible* kind of mood.

We'd tried at first to get into a Russian restaurant across the street, only a few blocks from our hotel in the seventh arrondisement. (We always have stayed in the seventh district — in different hotels but always along Rue Cler, because that street has a food market. That way Lisa can get up early in the morning and go down to select fresh items for her breakfast … and I can do what I perceive to be a key requirement of any vacation: sleep.)

Inside the Russian restaurant were a handful of servers … and absolutely no customers. One of the servers asked if we had a reservation. I looked around. At that moment I couldn't recall the exact phrase for "Are you kidding?" in French.

So we wandered across the way to a tiny Rumanian eatery that indeed was serving a few patrons. At the door, I performed one of my favorite tasks while in Paris — asking for a table ("Une table pour deux, s'il vous plaît, madame?"), which ranks near the top with cashing traveler's checks ("Puis-je encaisser un cheque de voyage ici?").

It was dark inside, and as our eyes adjusted we could see this was truly a tiny restaurant — tiny in a city *known* for tiny restaurants.

Now, yes, it is a fact service in Europe is generally slow by American standards. After all, monsieur and madame, you are supposed to *savor* the dining experience.

But in this establishment I noted that after we had been waiting a good twenty-five minutes, we still had not received anything beyond our beverages.

More tables filled up. And, as everyone in Paris believes cigarettes to be not only handed down but ordained by God himself, the air was becoming thick with smoke.

On the other hand, the music being piped in over the speaker system — American pop — had been changed over to what we presumed was Rumanian. So we sat back — or as far back as we could move at our very small table — and waited.

And waited.

The challenge for the restaurant servers, we noticed, was now becoming one of circumnavigating the crowded tables. The help, it appeared, consisted entirely of a mother, who was also the cook, and her daughter. They began passing miniature baskets of bread over customers' heads.

The father then arrived, saw so many people did not have their entrées and began yelling at his daughter. (As I say, we speak no Rumanian, but we could get the gist of his message.)

Before he started taking orders, though, he switched on a video cassette recorder and television that rested on a little refrigerator along the far wall. He turned up the volume, and into view came a somewhat matronly woman, dressed in gown and tiara, who began singing in Rumanian.

He did not turn off the music from the overhead speaker.

More people crowded in. More cigarette smoke. More jostling.

Still no food.

Then in through the front marched twenty-four — I counted them — men and women of various ages. The older man at the front end of the line — it was so jampacked in there by then, the newcomers had to stay in a line, from the front door to the back kitchen door — held up his left hand and loudly proclaimed something that sounded like, "Bros kenacuff, ad mendin ma dinkenuff."

And with that, all twenty-four burst into boisterous song, what we took for Christmas caroles in Rumanian.

Mind you, the TV was still on, the elderly woman still singing and the overhead speaker was still blaring away.

At the end of the song, some diners applauded, many continued the shouted conversations they'd tried to maintain throughout the entertainment.

More customers came in. More smoke. Still no food.

The lead singer announced another song, and again his troupe burst into their rendition of … whatever it was they were singing.

Somewhere around their fourth or fifth song — the mother occasionally would pop her head out around the kitchen door, frown, then retreat — five musicians, with horns and, I swear, an accordion, entered. Or as best they could. Two couldn't squeeze in and had to stand in the doorway, propping open the door.

The carolers cheered. Then the two dozen singers and the five musicians joined forces and launched into more very emphatic music. The waitress — the owners' daughter — by this time abandoned any pretense at serving tables and started taking photos of one of the musicians in particular. Her boyfriend, no doubt, given how she beamed at him.

Soon beer was handed out to the carolers and the racket resumed.

I've no idea how long it was before we received our food. I do remember the carolers were still there when he managed to extract ourselves from the restaurant.

I couldn't even tell you what I had to eat. But I doubt the meal caused the headache I had as we stumbled back to our hotel.

~

For the record, I did not want the tart. I said at the time I did not want the tart. "Non," I said.

But Lisa clearly desired something or other to go with her coffee and, she said, you like rhubarb and we're on vacation after all.

So we ordered the tart. Lisa asked for the cheese platter for her and the rhubarb tart for me.

The waiter brought the cheese platter and an apple tart. Lisa noticed. She made him take back the apple tart and bring the rhubarb.

This is what Lisa and I later referred to as tempting fate. We had messed with the time lines.

After we finished our coffee and food, we took a bus to our hotel on Avenue de la Motte-Picquet. I recall it was raining. I also recall that the bus had moved merely a few blocks from the café when my stomach started to lurch. And then it churned. Then I started feeling these repeated, sharp stabbing pains.

By the time we arrived at our hotel, I was sick. Really, verily sick.

Now you should know I hardly ever become ill. Practically never. And lord knows I've ingested all sorts of manner of things over the years and not been affected. (Well, no more than intended.)

But that night was awful. I did not go to the hospital, but it was under serious consideration, let me tell you.

Before morning we concluded I was suffering from food poisoning. Lisa noted that the infamous rhubarb tart back at the café had had a custard base, and that it must have "gone bad," as she said … as if we were discussing some wayward cousin of mine.

A day or so later I was feeling somewhat better. That is, I could stand upright. But I still wasn't up for eating anything. (I wasn't to have another full meal for a couple weeks, in fact.)

We went out for short strolls, but — having essentially no energy whatsoever — I mostly sat down every chance that happened along.

By Saturday, our last full day in Paris, I managed to eat a half of a piece of bread.

But also by that time — as if by some cruel weird-beyond-belief fool trick — Lisa had developed what we later learned was the flu. We don't really know how, but there we were.

The weather had cleared and, as it was apparent Lisa was going to sleep all day and there was little I could do for her, I recalled I had seen along les Champs earlier in the week (before our vacation fiasco struck) that the newly released movie *Shadow of the Vampire* — *L'Ombre du Vampire* — with Willem

Dafoe was playing and, even better, that it was in English with French subtitles.

So, bidding adieu to my sleeping spouse, I dragged myself over to the nearby metro stop and rode over to les Champs.

In Paris, at least along les Champs, the booths where they sell movie tickets aren't necessarily where the actual movie house is. So I bought my ticket at the booth, sat down to rest for about twenty minutes or so, then went up the street several doors until I found the actual salon.

There was no one at the entrance, so I pushed my way in. Down this long hall, around a bend, down another long hall. And there, at the far end, I could see a concession stand and the same garcon who had sold me my ticket earlier. He seemed to be waiting just for me, smiling, and he motioned for me to come ahead: "Ici, monsieur."

He tore my ticket and pointed to a door at the other end of the room. So I went through and walked down this narrow hallway that went on and on, turning slightly every so often.

I noticed it definitely was going downhill, and getting narrower. I also became aware of it getting darker, as there were less light bulbs the farther I went. Soon, there was no light at all, and I actually could touch both sides of the hall without stretching my arms out hardly at all.

Eventually I could see in the distance a diminutive rectangle of light, at slightly below eye level. I kept walking … and banged *smack* into what I came to understand was the door to the actual movie house auditorium itself. After some thought, I pushed it open, went in and sat down.

Very soon, the lights went down and commercials started, about twenty minutes worth (I timed them), mostly with tanned young naked women selling all manner of innocent things — wristwatches, automobiles. Then the lights went back up and we waited another fifteen minutes or so for the movie finally to commence.

On the way back our hotel, I realized it was getting on to rush hour, as this was a Saturday and in the full clutch of Christmas shopping. The metro trains were packed — I mean, the platforms were completely full, people were mobbed way up back even onto the stairwells and it seemed no one got off the trains, and you had to push and squeeze to get on.

Which I managed to do eventually. But a few stops later, a quartet of Italians somehow made their way onto the crush of my car — I knew they were Italians because they actually said "mama mia" — and started shoving. There wasn't much room for this sort of behavior and, as I was weak from not eating in days, I was starting to feel dizzy again.

Our train jumped forward, moving through the tunnel. The shouting and pushing resumed and the inevitable happened, as we knew it would: With a second jolt of the train, a whole wave of passengers fell backward — WHAM — domino-like, and down I went, helplessly sandwiched among them.

Some kind Parisians propped me up. Which was fortunate as I was considering up until that moment that maybe the whole thing was an hallucination.

Somehow I slowly but not necessarily surely trudged back to our hotel. Lisa was awake and I told her of my adventure. I was not certain she believed me.

We have returned to Paris since that food-poisoning occurrence. And we've had a great time.

But I stay away from those French tarts. And I advise you to do the same.

Chapter Seventeen
The Fur Does Fly

I had not seen it as a trap at the time, but that's what it was, intentional or not. When we bought this house I lost my last excuse for our not having a pet.

In the past, I had been able to present a rational legal defense: "Yes, dear, I know it doesn't say so specifically in our rental agreement, but I'm fairly certain our landlord wouldn't be happy if we kept a llama in our apartment ...."

But after about a year in this big house, it became increasingly clear we were destined to have animals as intentional co-inhabitants.

Don't misunderstand: I like animals. I give to all the right charities. Most of my life I've have had dogs or cats, and sometimes both at the same time, as pets. But somewhere around about 1986 or so, when the last pet advocate with whom I was sharing living quarters moved out, I noticed something remarkable: I could breath again. As time went on, my sinuses cleared and it was a brand new world.

From then on, I've resisted any long-term living arrangements with creatures possessing fur and dander. (Only people without allergies contend there are such things as mammals that won't bother your sinuses.)

And besides, don't we homeowners have enough to take care of, what with leaves to rake or snow to shovel, gutters to clear and all the other day-to-day tragedies — planned and otherwise — that occur?

Then came that day at a flea market in Paw Paw when my wife spied the guy selling bunnies, and I knew my unimpaired-breathing days were ended.

In the two years since, Chloe (or *Mister* Chloe, as he became known, after certain until-then unexpected discoveries were made) pretty much has taken over the first floor of our house. It is his domain.

In the tribe to which he sees himself belonging, Chloe — despite weighing only slightly more than four pounds — considers himself top bunny. He is, if you will, the Alpha Bunny. Lisa is clearly identified as his maternal figure.

I, on the other, have no authority whatsoever.

Chloe generally is pleasant and even-tempered. When he's especially happy, he does his bunny dance of joy, galloping about and wagging his head. Sometimes he grooms *us*.

He generally is fairly social and, as a result, has had his portrait painted — no, really — and a local documentary film maker put together a three-minute feature of Chloe's day. (I've been told "Notes From on the Ground" will be available for rent soon at a video store in town.)

On the other hand, he's been known to hold a grudge for a very long time. Once, a full half an hour after I'd accidentally startled him while hurrying to answer the telephone, he came up behind me while I was sitting on the floor and bit me. Startled, I turned around and he there sat, unrepentant, as if to say, See, that'll show you.

When I've tried to lure him into his cage at night, sometimes he'll pull back his ears, hunch his back and stare at me, from his perch atop the ottoman in the living room. His meaning is evident: You're not the bunny of me.

A couple weeks ago we had delivered what the store referred to as an entertainment tower. And I admit, it was much taller than it had appeared at the store.

"Everybody says that," the two delivery guys laughed in unison. And then, placing said entertainment tower in the middle of our living room, they left.

As the thing was still on its moving casters, I slid it into a corner of the room with only a bit of difficulty, then squeezed behind it and placed our television set, VCR and tape rewinder on its shelves. In doing so, though, its weight must have shifted, as the space I'd left to slip back out between the tower and the corner wall now was somewhat narrower than when I'd squeaked in. That is to say, narrower than I was ....

When I finally managed to extricate myself, some 15 minutes later, I let Chloe out of his cage. He immediately dashed into the living room to examine this new piece of furniture — this was, after all, not something he'd approved for his living quarters.

In no time, he'd found his way around to the back of tower, where he promptly began tugging on the TV and VCR electrical cords that were plugged into the wall. The cords long ago had been wrapped in plastic to prevent the rabbit from fricasseeing himself, but I feared he'd rip the cable out of the wall.

I politely asked him to come out of there. (Yes, sometimes he'll come when called, if he's so inclined. He has a vocabulary of approximately eight words and actually can count to two. Really.) But he just kept yanking on the cords, even harder now, just to demonstrate who was boss.

As there was no easy way I could get back there to retrieve him, I took a broom, reached over and behind the TV and tried to gently swat him out. It took a couple tries, but I managed to convince him.

Minutes later, of course, he charged right back and gave those cords more of a workout. I took the broom and pushed him out again. And he hopped right back ....

Lisa came home, saw the situation and wedged a pillow between the tower and the wall. Chloe dashed over to the pillow, studied it for a moment and, being a rabbit and all, hopped on top of it, then back behind the tower.

So up from the basement I brought a empty cardboard box and an old blanket. We coerced Chloe back out again, and I pushed the box and the pillow in the gap on one side. The blanket I stuffed along the other side, between the tower and the fireplace, just for good measure.

Chloe had been in the kitchen while I did this — Lisa had been distracting him with dandelions or something. But the second he finished his snack, he zoomed back into the living room to once more try to gain access behind the tower, clearly for some unknown reason now his favorite place in his universe.

But the pillow-box barricade apparently was too high. He reared up on his hind legs. He tried to pull the pillow out with his teeth. He clawed on the box. He tried the other side, and tugged on the blanket. He ran back to the first corner and worked some more.

He was, in a word, furious. And then — even though he had not seen *me* put any of these impediments in place — this four-plus-pound white bunny turned toward me, pulled back his ears … and glared. This undoubtedly was all *my* fault.

It's now been many days since the entertainment tower arrived. And several times a day, Chloe still tries to get back behind it, giving the cardboard box a tentative scratch or a brief tug on the pillow, to no avail.

And then, to ensure I haven't missed the point, he hops over to me, ears cocked, and you can tell he's thinking: Someday, maybe not today, maybe not tomorrow, but someday, when you least expect it, I'll get back there again. And then you'll see. You're not the bunny of me.

Chapter Eighteen

Tales From the Home Front: Winter Again
Homeland Security

Don't get me wrong. We have nothing against squirrels. My wife even owns one of those cute T-shirts showing a portrait of a cuddly brown squirrel, under the heading: *Wanted in Three Neighborhoods.*

And when we used to see that charming little chipmunk scurrying into and out of our garage through the tiniest of holes near the door, we thought, oh, that's OK, what can he hurt?

During our first winter in this house, after that heavy snowfall, we'd occasionally see his head pop up above the snow as he'd quickly orient himself, like a character in a Bugs Bunny cartoon, then drop back back down out of sight as he made his way home.

And even when we first heard the patter of little pawsteps somewhere up in the attic late in the evening, we were not concerned. Hey, it's a big, old house, we thought. We can share.

But then two things happened recently. One afternoon, some kind of creature — something with teeth and claws — tried unsuccessfully to make its way up through a heating vent in the floor. I wasn't there, but it was variously described by my wife as anywhere in size between that of a small field mouse and that of, say, a wildebeest.

We closed a number of the vents, put on sweaters and hoped for the best.

A number of weeks later, I was standing in the living room one quiet afternoon when I heard a sudden clawing racket that sounded for all the world like a jackhammer being applied, with some hostility, to the ceiling right over my head.

I hammered on the wall and the noise stopped immediately … for about a minute. I pounded on the wall again, then dashed upstairs, checking in the closets, up in the attic and the crawlspace. No luck — the villains had fled.

They came back, of course, on a daily basis. They were overrunning our attic, and loudly. These were the Taliban of squirrels, and countermeasures were required.

So I telephoned the local franchise of a national pest-control business. But the person there said they didn't handle squirrels.

Why not, I asked. Your advertisement says you do rodents. What's the difference? They both have fur, four legs and a tail.

She replied that she wasn't certain … but "maybe it's because rodents are nocturnal?"

She referred me to a business locally with a name something like Critter Cowboys or some such. The fellow there, while very pleasant, said this was the busy time of year for squirrels — who would have thought — and, besides, he was getting ready to go out of town for a — I'm not making this up — for an animal-control convention. ("And here you see in our PowerPoint presentation that the squirrel possesses sharp front teeth, equally good for chewing nuts as well as biting through telephone cable ….)

He did give me the name, however, of a guy he knew who handles squirrels part time. Because it was pretty clear what I truly needed now was a Squirrel Professional.

The Squirrel Professional indeed had that seasoned Dan'l Boone look about him — more than a few years of experience — when he showed up with battered squirrel cages in one hand and a jar of generic-brand peanut butter in the other.

I took Eddie up into the attic, which is accessible only by climbing up a slim ladder built into the side of one of our bedroom closets and through a narrow gap at the top.

Once up there, he examined the premises, meditatively rolling discarded acorn shells he found in the crawlspace between his fingers, as if he were divining not only the squirrels' motives, coloring and gender, but their Social Security numbers, voting preferences and favorite hockey teams, too.

He set the traps and said he'd see me in about three days.

Sure enough, come Monday evening there arose such a racket from upstairs I first thought our house was being shelled by cannon fire.

In the echoing crawlspace I found an extremely agitated red squirrel, caught in one of the cages and shaking it so ferociously it reminded me of the TV set in the old *Calvin and Hobbes* comic strip, where it would actually lift itself straight up off its stand.

I telephoned Eddie, and about a half hour later he arrived and calmly took our captive out to his truck, promising to drive it out to be released, on its own recognizance in a friend's woods.

(As Eddie's contract called for payment of $35 a squirrel, I briefly wondered if maybe it wouldn't be in his better interest to let the creature go, about two doors away, figuring it would find its way back to our attic to be captured all over again. As if I'd be able to identify one red squirrel from another.

(I also asked if — as it's $35 for squirrels — if he charged less for, say, chipmunks, as they're smaller. He replied they were all the same.)

The next night, at about the same time, there was another crash from the attic, as loud as if a car had run into the side of the house. But this time when I got up there the cages stood empty, all their doors tripped and shut.

Eddie returned and, sheet metal and drill under his arm, disappeared into the dark recesses of our attic's crawlspace, searching for a possible entry/exit point. After a couple minutes, his voice drifted out, "Oh, my goodness. You'd better look at this."

I cautiously followed his voice, trying not to hit my head on the beams, back into the enemies' lair. And there, not far from the north wall and banked up against a pile of insulation, were more acorn shells than you'd find in the Meijer produce department on a good Saturday morning.

Oh, my goodness.

Once Eddie had affixed the sheet metal — or whatever highly professional materials he was using — and sprayed the space around it with something, he said, squirrels didn't like the taste of very much (which, it turned out, was rust proofing), he left, noting we should keep a couple of the cages in place — just to make sure.

After all, no more squirrels should be able to get into the house, right?

So I established a routine: Every morning, afternoon and evening, flashlight in hand, I'd climb up the ladder into the attic, exhale, then gingerly open the crawlspace door and peer in. No squirrels meant it was a good day to be alive. For us *and* the squirrels, now safely barred from regaining entry into the house.

But after about the third day I noticed that, though the cage doors were still open and the traps unsprung, the little mounds of peanut butter that Eddie had left inside them were getting … smaller. I looked again. Yep, they definitely were smaller than they were yesterday.

I called Eddie.

Upon his reexamination of the crime scene, he determined we had a second, different culprit. The peanut butter that had lured the squirrels to their capture was now attracting mice.

So he added some cheese (no, I don't know what variety) and a very efficient-looking glue board, which is exactly what you think it is: a board with glue on it.

The next morning, I climbed back up, exhaled and peeked into the crawlspace. Empty cage, vacant glue board. Less cheese.

It was time for some lateral thinking. Thinking outside the cage, so to speak.

That's when I remembered the pair of plastic mouse-trap box things I'd purchased not long after we'd moved into this house. The kind mice enter by pushing down the stubby spring one-way door at one side to get at the bait inside the box, but then they can't get back out. The mice then wait there until you carry the box outside to set them free.

The boxes were quite roomy, too, for a solitary mouse — *"Atrapa hasta 4 ratones,"* it said reassuringly on the outside of the box.

(I had asked the clerks at the hardware store before I bought these boxes how we could be so certain the mice couldn't escape. What if, I reasoned, what if one mouse held down the trap door while its accomplice scurried inside to retrieve the bait …? The clerks just looked at each other, then back at me, without answering.)

I brought one of the boxes up from the basement, slid back the lid and dropped in a dollop of organic peanut butter. Then I took it up to the crawlspace and placed it gently next to the glue board and the squirrel cage.

Within an hour we had our man … or mouse. A tiny field mouse, with dark almost black fur and very large eyes.

Once I'd carried the box out to the back yard and set it down next to the flowering cherry tree, I opened the lid. The field mouse popped its head up out of the top and looked at me. I explained that I was setting it free, unharmed, but in exchange it had to promise not to ever come back inside our house.

The rodent looked at me, turned around to the tree, looked back at me … then leaped out of the box and ran off away from house.

All was right with the world.

~

After about two more weeks of silence up in the attic, and no sightings of squirrel or mouse, I telephoned Eddie to inform him he could come to recover his traps and submit his bill. He'd done a splendid job.

The following Saturday I clambered back up the ladder to the attic, bearing with me my usual trusty flashlight, a pair of gloves and a discarded paper grocery bag to hold all the acorns and shells abandoned by the Taliban squirrels in the crawlspace.

It took me maybe twenty minutes or more to gather up all the nuts and detritus left behind. Some of the acorns had been wedged in pretty tightly into the crevices and corners.

As I was reaching for what was likely the last of the acorns packed along the far wall — I was lying across a sheet of fluffy pink insulation that rested on a slab of wood that in turn was placed across two of the forty-five-degree beams — when I heard this hissing sound, not far from my right ear.

Air escaping, I thought, but from what? The insulation?

I paid no more attention and stretched out my left arm again to scoop up those remaining acorns, in doing so also unintentionally pushing my body down against the insulation.

And I heard that hissing again. It sounded as if it were coming from *beneath* the insulation.

Without moving from off the slab of wood on which I was lying, I peeled back the upper part of the insulation. The hissing became louder and more insistent.

And that's when I was suddenly confronted with two rows of very pointed, very shiny, very angry teeth. About three inches from my nose.

I'm sure I uttered something along the lines of *Yiiikes* as I sprang away — all the way back outside the crawlspace into the attic proper. (This leap backward was very similar, as I recall, to when I once finally and somewhat dramatically got a rather temperamental gas oven back in my apartment in Columbus to light — and, with a BOOM, the next thing I knew I was lying in the living room.)

As I cautiously peeked my head around the crawlspace door, I could see my assailant. It really wasn't so large after all, as it continued hissing, and slowly — like those jerky-moving mechanical monsters at an amusement park haunted house in the 1950s — withdrew back into the darkness of the woodwork.

But not before I noticed under its front legs what surely must have been wings.

I called Eddie.

The two of us spent a good forty-five minutes pulling up the layers of pink insulation in the crawlspace. After all, with its exit now covered up, this bat would have no way to get out of the house once its winter hibernation period ended.

But we had no luck. Not a creature was stirring.

Besides, Eddie said, with his experience he'd *know* if there were a bat in this house. "I can *smell* 'em," he declared.

There were, he said, no bats residing here, asleep or awake. Ever.

Each night after that, for a good several weeks, I'd lie in bed, secure in the notion that our old attic was critter-free.

But I kept one ear cocked in that direction, just the same.

Michael Chevy Castranova these days is editor of the national-award-winning *Business Direct Weekly*, the only weekly business-to-business newspaper covering all twelve counties of western Michigan. (There, there's that plug in early.)

Over the years he has worked as a cartoonist, a freelance tennis instructor, a high school English teacher, in a bank, on a freight dock and at a couple department stores, as a newspaper reporter and as a magazine editor and as a movie and restaurant reviewer. Among other things.

Michael has won awards for his writing, including from the International Association of Business Communicators.

He lives in a relatively old house — old enough for someone whose idea of how to repair anything starts with a search for the Yellow Pages — with his wife, Lisa Williams, and their rabbit, Mr. Chloe, who can count to two.

To order additional copies call the Kalamazoo Gazette at 1-269-388-2710 or visit the Gazette store at www.gazettestore.com